SCIENTIFIC AMERICAN EXPLORES BIG IDEAS

Immune System Hacks

Published in 2023 by Scientific American Educational Publishing
in association with **The Rosen Publishing Group**
29 East 21st Street, New York, NY 10010

Contains material from Scientific American®, a division of Springer Nature America, Inc., reprinted by permission as well as original material from Rosen Publishing Group®.

First Edition

Scientific American
Lisa Pallatroni: Custom Book Editor

Rosen Publishing
Daniel R. Faust: Compiling Editor
Michael Moy: Senior Graphic Designer

Cataloging-in-Publication Data
Names: Scientific American, Inc.
Title: Immune system hacks / edited by the Editors of Scientific American.
Description: New York : Scientific American Educational Publishing, 2023. | Series: Scientific American explores big ideas | Includes glossary and index.
Identifiers: ISBN 9781684169306 (pbk.) | ISBN 9781684169313 (library bound) | ISBN 9781684169320 (ebook)
Subjects: LCSH: Immune system–Juvenile literature. | Immunity–Juvenile literature. | Natural immunity–Juvenile literature.
Classification: LCC QR181.8 I668 2023 | DDC 616.07'9–dc23

Manufactured in the United States of America

Cover: sorbetto/iStock.com
Websites listed were live at the time of publication

CPSIA Compliance Information: Batch #SACS23.
For further information, contact Rosen Publishing at 1-800-237-9932.

CONTENTS

INTRODUCTION

Most of us probably never think about our immune system until we get sick. Runny noses, coughs, fever, and fatigue are all signs that your immune system is at work trying to fight off an infection. But sometimes our immune system needs help. Vaccines train our immune system to recognize and kill foreign viruses and bacteria before they can make us sick.

The articles in this book provide an overview of the human immune system, encompassing not just the basic principles behind it but also the ways in which our immune system might malfunction and how scientists have worked to improve the way it functions, including vaccines and immunotherapy. Section 1, "Boosting Our Immune System," looks at how scientists have discovered ways to improve the way our immune system protects us from disease and infection. It addresses the particularly polarizing debate about vaccines and whether they are truly safe. Section 2, "Fighting Yourself: Autoimmune Disorders," examines what happens when someone's immune system malfunctions and treats an otherwise healthy body part like it's an infection. Section 3, "Hacking a Cure for Cancer and Other Diseases," takes readers into the lab to look at the various ways scientists and researchers are trying to hack the immune system to treat diseases like cancer, diabetes, and Alzheimer's disease. Section 4, "Hacking COVID: The Search for a Vaccine," looks at the recent fight against COVID-19 and the struggle to find a vaccine that would stem the spread of the global pandemic that recently brought the world to a halt. Section 5, "Future Hacks: Learning from COVID," turns its eyes to the future and discusses how the response to COVID-19–including the fear, misinformation, and conspiracy theories surrounding both the pandemic and the vaccines and treatments devised to combat it–could have a negative impact on our fight against future pandemics.

Section 1: Boosting Our Immune System

How to Boost Your Immunity

By Claudia Wallis

Fear and fraud often travel together. As coronavirus anxiety began to spread across the land, so did bogus nostrums promising protection from this modern-day plague. As early as March 6, 2020, U.S. regulators began to issue warnings to companies promoting false claims, such as this one touting the benefits of drinking a daily dose of silver particles: "It's actually widely acknowledged in both science and the medical industry that ionic silver kills coronaviruses." Um, no.

For people who hope to build up their resistance to coronavirus and infections of all kinds, there are no magic formulas—but there are some science-based steps one can take to maintain a healthy immune system. For starters, don't smoke. Cigarette smokers are much more vulnerable to respiratory infections. Second, make sure you are covering all your nutritional bases with a wide variety of vegetables, fruits, and other elements of a healthy diet. "Eating an optimal diet reduces the risk of getting an infection and reduces the severity of infections," says Wafaie Fawzi, professor of nutrition, epidemiology, and global health at Harvard University's T. H. Chan School of Public Health. Third, practice good sleep hygiene so you can raise your chances of adequate nightly rest. And fourth, get regular exercise, which will also help you sleep.

On the dietary front, several nutrients have been tied to improved resistance to viruses. Taking zinc supplements, for example, has been linked to a reduced rate of respiratory infections and shorter duration of related symptoms. Deficiency in zinc, a mineral found in meat, shellfish, nuts, and whole grains, is more prevalent in less developed countries, Fawzi notes, but it can occur in wealthier nations, especially during a time of high unemployment and disruptions to the food supply chain.

Vitamins C and D have also been shown to improve resistance to respiratory infections. Perhaps relevant to COVID-19, vitamin

C plays a role in reducing tissue damage from our own immune responses. Oral doses of the vitamin have also been shown to shorten the amount of time in an ICU and on a ventilator for heart surgery patients, according to a 2019 meta-analysis. Could it help COVID patients? Researchers are looking at it, Fawzi says.

As for vitamin D, a 2017 meta-analysis of 25 randomized controlled trials found that vitamin D supplements cut the risk of acute respiratory infection—especially for people with low levels of the vitamin, which is about 40 percent of Americans. The percentage is far higher in Black Americans and Hispanics. Fawzi points out that late winter/early spring, when the pandemic began in the U.S., happens to be when D levels are especially low because we acquire the nutrient mainly via sun exposure.

Fawzi and his colleagues are investigating whether vitamin D might help COVID patients. In the meantime, he suggests taking a basic multivitamin. "A supplement with the recommended daily allowances of vitamins and minerals would be prudent," he says, along with a balanced diet. It might particularly help elderly adults, who are prone to nutritional deficiencies.

As for sleep, scientists have long known that it plays an essential role in bolstering our defenses. Studies show that if you deprive people of sleep after administering a vaccine, they will produce a weaker antibody response than folks who slept. Research suggests that sleep enhances the migration of T cells to the lymph nodes, where they are presented with foreign molecules that trigger antibody production, explains neuroscientist Luciana Besedovsky, who investigates sleep and the immune system at Ludwig Maximilian University of Munich in Germany.

A 2015 study that measured average sleep duration for 164 healthy volunteers and then dripped a rhinovirus into their nose found that those who slept six or fewer hours a night were four times as likely to develop a cold as those who slept more than seven hours. Similarly, a study that followed 57,000 women found that those who slept five or fewer hours nightly were 40 percent more likely to have developed pneumonia over a four-year study period than eight-hour sleepers. Prolonged sleep loss, Besedovsky says, can create a state of low-grade inflammation: "This seems to exhaust your immune system in the long run, so that it may not be able to fight infections that well."

Committing to a regular bedtime and nightly routine that helps you sleep, along with a healthy diet–and perhaps a multivitamin–will not necessarily keep the coronavirus at bay. But these steps have a true silver lining of helping you endure whatever health threats blow your way.

About the Author

Claudia Wallis is an award-winning science journalist whose work has appeared in the New York Times, Time, Fortune, *and the* New Republic. *She was science editor at* Time *and managing editor of* Scientific American Mind.

Fact or Fiction?: Vaccines Are Dangerous

By Dina Fine Maron

The world greets newborn babies by bombarding them with everything from dust to disease-causing microbes. Babies can deftly parry exposures to certain harmful substances, thanks to antibodies passed on to them in the womb. But this kind of inherited immunity is short-lived, so a child must develop their own immune system response to combat life-threatening diseases. That's where vaccines come into the picture. By age two, most children will receive almost 30 shots designed to boost a child's natural defenses against disease. Yet at the same time, parents who take their children for those recommended vaccinations might be inundated with website- and celebrity-espoused rumors making false claims that shots are not necessary or cause autism.

At best, navigating this landscape can be confusing. But when weighing the risks of encountering life-threatening disease against the benefits of receiving a vaccine, there's no contest. The vast majority of children do not experience anything worse than short-lived redness or itching at the spot of the injection. So why is there so much misinformation?

One reason is developmental timing. Children receive a bevy of vaccines before age two, roughly overlapping with when children with autism spectrum disorder may noticeably develop symptoms, such as the inability to gain new skills. That coincidence has helped the autism-vaccine connection myth persist. And what may have once been passed around by neighborhood gossip is now amplified worldwide by websites and social media. But the science simply does not bear out such fears. In August 2011 the Institute of Medicine (IOM) released a report that examined eight childhood vaccines and potential side effects. It found that vaccines are largely safe and that side effects are usually very rare and minor.

Side Effects

The overwhelming medical evidence finds that most vaccine side effects among newborns and young children are mild—swelling, redness, and a small, hard lump at the site of the injection—and typically pass within a couple of days. A far less common but serious vaccine side effect, occurring in fewer than one in a million cases, is an immediate allergic reaction that can be treated with common medications to ease itching or swelling or, in more serious cases, by administering epinephrine. Rarely, with certain vaccinations, there can be other problems. After receiving the first shot of the measles-mumps-rubella (MMR) vaccination, for example, a child has a roughly one in 3,000 chance of developing a fever that leads to a seizure. Such seizures do not lead to any permanent neurological damage. Moreover, they also occur more generally when kids develop high fevers—afflicting up to 5 percent of young children. That does not mean it is not upsetting to see. "It's hard to watch your child seize," says Paul Offit, a pediatrics professor at Children's Hospital of Philadelphia. His own daughter had a seizure after receiving the combo vaccine against diphtheria, tetanus, and pertussis, but he says it's important to remember that this type of seizure does not cause long-term consequences. And scientific evidence finds that MMR-related seizures are actually less frequent than ones that occur as a direct result of the measles infection itself.

What's In a Vaccine?

When a person encounters a pathogen, there is no way to predict whether it will induce a mild or severe form of disease or how the body will react. But vaccines are selected to contain a weakened or dead form of the disease-causing germ that can spark an immune response. Exposure will thus allow the body to build up immunity in a controlled way. The immune system reaction stops this compromised foreign invader in its tracks at the site of injection. And the key to vaccine success is that, afterward, the immune system starts to create fast-response infection fighters called memory cells that will circulate throughout the body and be able to recognize (and fend off) that same pathogen in the future.

These weak or killed stimulants, called antigens, are grown in a lab setting, isolated, and then mixed with preservatives, stabilizers, and a substance like aluminum that will trigger the immune system to vigorously respond to the vaccine. The process saves lives: among children born in the past two decades, vaccinations will prevent more than 20 million hospitalizations and 732,000 deaths, according to U.S. Centers for Disease Control and Prevention estimates.

Why Do Vaccines Cause Any Side Effects?

Like any medicine, immunizations can lead to a negative reaction. That's not surprising because every individual is different. Genetic variations, immune deficiencies, and environmental exposures all contribute to how a person's body reacts to inoculations against disease.

Is Such a High Number of Shots Dangerous?

Expert medical bodies, including the American Academy of Pediatrics (AAP), urge parents to vaccinate their kids against 16 diseases. The CDC schedule for childhood vaccinations, which relies on recommendations from the Advisory Committee on Immunization Practices and is endorsed by the AAP, is drawn up based on data detailing when the body's immune system will mount the best response to the vaccine, balanced against the need to protect kids at the earliest age possible. There are no scientific data suggesting a medical benefit from spacing out vaccines over a longer period than the official recommendations.

Vaccines are also regularly evaluated for safety. Before they are added to the recommended regimen, they must undergo testing to make sure they won't interfere with one another. Multiple studies have also evaluated vaccines' cumulative effects.

Still, pediatricians face continual pressure from some worried parents who may want to spread out the recommended inoculations or postpone certain vaccinations, decisions that can prolong the period of vulnerability to disease. For example, a nationally representative study published in the April 2015 *Pediatrics* found that in an average month, 93 percent of surveyed doctors received at least one request from parents to spread out shots. And it happened fairly frequently: over a fifth of the 534 surveyed physicians reported that 10 percent of parents made such requests. Parents' wishes were then often honored–most of the surveyed clinicians ultimately agreed to do so, at least some of the time.

Yet fears about a child's body not being able to handle potent vaccines are misguided. Children's immune systems respond to several hundred foreign substances that trigger an immune response every day. In contrast, the complete schedule of recommended childhood vaccinations includes less than 200 antigens.

Do Vaccines Cause Autism?

Some concerns about vaccines stem from discredited work that suggested they lead to autism. (The findings were subsequently retracted, and the physician who did that small study was barred from practicing medicine because of ethical lapses.) More than a dozen studies have added to the body of evidence that this link does not exist. Expert groups, including the IOM and the AAP, agree that vaccines do not contribute to children's autism rates. The vaccine additive thimerosal, a preservative that contains a form of mercury (organomercurcial, not methylmercury) also does not cause autism. It is now only included in pediatric vaccines in trace amounts (or not at all), but there is no medical evidence that it causes autism in patients.

Can't Children Thrive Without Vaccines?

We live in a crowded, fast-moving world, and disease travels easily. The data are clear: failure to immunize a child comes with a much more formidable risk–leaving children vulnerable to contracting a potentially debilitating or lethal illness. Some children are too sick or too young to receive inoculations, so they remain at risk. If those children or other unvaccinated kids come into contact with someone else who was not protected against certain microbes, that can set off a wave of disease such as the measles outbreak in the U.S. in the summer of 2017. Maladies that have become uncommon, such as polio and measles, can also quickly reappear if we stop vaccinating against them, particularly when they are unintentionally imported across geographic borders. The 2015 measles outbreak that rippled through the U.S., for example, had genetic markers that suggest it came from an overseas traveler. Protecting kids actually helps protect everyone.

About the Author

Dina Fine Maron, formerly an associate editor at Scientific American, *is now a wildlife trade investigative reporter at* National Geographic.

The Brain Has a Special Kind of Memory for Past Infections

By Raleigh McElvery

While the brain and spinal cord have their own squad of specialized immune cells, the peripheral immune system is armed with a larger battalion of proteins, cells, and entire organs, such as the spleen, that ward off invaders. Over the past decade, researchers have made great progress in understanding how the peripheral immune system affects neural activity: how immune signals that originate outside the central nervous system can affect cognitive processes, social behavior, neurodegeneration, and more. In fact, they have learned that immune cells from the periphery routinely patrol the central nervous system and support its function. In a recent study, researchers showed for the first time that—just as the brain remembers people, places, smells, and so on—it also stores what they call "memory traces" of the body's past infections. Reactivating the same brain cells that encode this information is enough to swiftly summon the peripheral immune system to defend at-risk tissues.

In some ways, this is not entirely a surprise. It is clear the peripheral immune system is capable of retaining information about past infections to fight off future ones—otherwise, vaccines would not work. But Asya Rolls, a neuroimmunologist at the Technion–Israel Institute of Technology and the paper's senior author, says the study expands this concept of classical immunological memory. Initially she was taken aback that the brain could store traces of immune activity and use them to trigger such a precise response. "I was amazed," she says.

Rolls's team focused on a brain region called the insular cortex, which senses the body's internal state through visceral signals such as temperature, pain, hunger, and—the researchers reasoned—perhaps immune activity. They studied strains of mice with a type of gut inflammation known as colitis and used fluorescent markers to take snapshots of the groups of brain cells in the insular cortex that became active during the infection.

After the infection and immune response dissipated, the researchers injected the mice with a drug that artificially reactivated those same groups of brain cells. They were stunned by what they saw: on reactivation, the insular cortex directed the immune system to mount a targeted response in the gut at the site of the original inflammation—even though, by that time, there was no infection, tissue damage, or pathogen-initiated local inflammation to be found. The brain had retained some sort of memory of the infection and was prepared to reinitiate the fight.

"This result was the one that kind of blew us away because we really didn't expect it," says the paper's first author, Tamar Koren of Technion. "This was, I think, our aha moment."

Repeating the experiments in mice that had abdominal cavity infections generated similar results. It remained unclear, however, how the insular cortex communicates with organs to spur an immune response.

To begin answering that question, the researchers used a fluorescent tracer to chart the nerve connections that allowed the brain to exchange messages with the gut and abdominal cavity. Koren suspects that this pathway is just one line of communication, however. She says the insular cortex could also be sending signals to the body's tissue linings or regulating hormone levels to help reactivate an immunological response.

Although there are likely additional brain regions at play, the insular cortex was the right place to start, says Kevin Tracey, president of the Feinstein Institutes for Medical Research and a neurosurgeon, who was not involved in the study. Tracey showed in the 1990s that a specific nerve connected to the brain stem could talk to peripheral immune cells and tamp down the immune response before it damaged the body. This phenomenon, now known as the inflammatory reflex, was the first evidence that neural circuitry could control the peripheral immune system. And it is now being used to treat autoimmune diseases such as rheumatoid arthritis.

The study provides "unassailable" evidence that the central nervous system can control the peripheral immune system, Tracey says. "It's an incredibly important contribution to the fields of neuroscience and immunology."

Just as researchers have traced sensory and motor processing to specific brain regions, Tracey suspects that a similar neurological "map" of immunological information also exists. This study, he says, is the first direct evidence of that map. "It's going to be really exciting to see what comes next," he adds.

Rolls's lab has begun devising clinical trials to treat chronic gut inflammation based on her team's findings. Many intestinal disorders, such as inflammatory bowel disease, are triggered by stress or strong emotions. The researchers think this causes neurons in the insular cortex to misfire, reactivating an immunological memory and triggering a misguided immune response. They were able to successfully alleviate colitis in mice by simply decreasing activation in the insular cortex, and they suspect that placing human patients in a functional magnetic resonance imaging machine and teaching them to consciously reduce activity in that region could relieve gut inflammation with less dependence on medication. Allowing the brain to respond instead, Rolls explains, would be the most balanced and personalized response her team could ask for.

About the Author

Raleigh McElvery is a science writer from Cambridge, Mass. Her background is in neuroscience, but she enjoys covering a wide variety of topics, from paleontology to astrophysics and everything in between.

Hidden Black Scientists Proved the Polio Vaccine Worked

By Ainissa Ramirez

In the summers of the early 1950s, multitudes of American children were stuck in their home. Parents didn't permit them to play together because, when the weather got warm, society entered a nightmare called polio. Children would eagerly begin their school breaks with a bicycle, scooter, or kite and end them in crutches, braces, or an iron lung.

The disease poliomyelitis, or polio, had been in the medical textbooks for decades. In the summers of the early 20th century, however, this illness grew into an epidemic. The virus behind the disease could infect anyone, but in the U.S., it caused the worst damage among children under five years old, and polio was consequently called infantile paralysis.

In early 1953 there was a glimmer of hope that this nightmare might come to an end. Medical researcher Jonas Salk created a polio vaccine that, when injected, stimulated the immune system to make antibodies that fought off the virus. By January of that year, he had inoculated 161 people, and the results looked promising. Salk's work was funded by the National Foundation for Infantile Paralysis (NFIP). This organization–founded in 1938 by polio sufferer and U.S. president Franklin Delano Roosevelt–evolved from a dilapidated spa in Warm Springs, Ga., for those afflicted with the disease to become a major polio research funder. Buoyed by Salk's early results, the NFIP, with its broad mission of conquering polio, started pushing to get hundreds of thousands of children vaccinated. But before moving ahead, Salk wanted to make sure his vaccine was the "safest and most certain" approach by monitoring the inoculation's ability to trigger enough antibodies to neutralize the virus. In earlier tests, monkeys were injected with the vaccine and monitored to see if they got sick, or their cells were observed to see if they deformed. But the number of the animals needed to test thousands of children was too costly and cumbersome.

Fortunately, researchers had found there were unique cells that could help. These were HeLa cells, the living line of cancer cells that were taken without permission from a Black patient named Henrietta Lacks years earlier. After blood was drawn from a vaccinated patient, part of it was placed in a glass dish along with HeLa cells and a small dose of polio. With those items, a microscopic–and deadly–battle commenced. In the dish, the poliovirus tried to attack the HeLa cells. If there were enough of the proper antibodies in the patient's blood, however, they blocked the virus from causing any harm. Scientists could readily see the cells under a microscope. If the HeLa cells looked misshapen, this meant that the right antibodies were not present in the blood.

To evaluate his vaccine, Salk would need tremendous amounts of HeLa cells. He would get help not from traditional established institutions such as Harvard University or Yale University but from a small Black college in the South that had become famous for cultivating peanuts.

In 1881 educator Booker T. Washington founded the Tuskegee Institute with 30 pupils inside an old church building in Alabama. Washington had big dreams for his small school, and they were realized. Just 50 years later, the number of students increased 100-fold. And the entire nation grew to know about this institute from botanist George Washington Carver's pioneering work on cultivating the peanut there. During World War II, the Tuskegee Airmen, an all-Black flying squadron, also put this sleepy part of the country on the map.

The NFIP had an old relationship with the Tuskegee Institute. In the 1940s, the NFIP funded the Tuskegee Infantile Paralysis Center, which not only supported the treatment of Black polio sufferers but also trained Black medical personnel for work back in their communities. This medical facility was one of the few polio centers that treated Black children because American hospitals were segregated. Even FDR's Warm Springs did not accept Black patients. In October 1952, looking ahead to polio vaccine testing, the NFIP's director of research, Harry Weaver, asked Russell W. Brown, director of the Carver Research Foundation at the Tuskegee Institute, to turn its halls into the world's first HeLa cell factory. Brown, who had a doctorate in bacterial physiology, was designated as the director of the project, and James (Jimmy) Henderson, a plant physiologist, assisted him. These Black men were asked to serve humanity in a time when their humanity was often denied. Not far from them, the infamous Tuskegee syphilis experiment was underway.

Both Brown and Henderson were solid scientists, but growing, storing, and maintaining HeLa cells had not been part of their technical training. That kind of expertise lay in a burgeoning field called tissue culture. Salk's proposed vaccine trial would require 10,000 glass tubes of HeLa cells every week from Tuskegee. William F. Scherer, a young postdoctoral researcher at the University of Minnesota, who did early work on the poliovirus using HeLa cells, had instructed students on this topic. He agreed to provide Brown and Henderson with the skills they needed. So on January 16, 1953, Brown and Henderson boarded a train in Alabama. And on January 18, 1953, they arrived in the frigid cold of Minnesota on their new mission.

In the 1950s, the Twin Cities of Minneapolis and Saint Paul, Minn., were segregated. Finding campus housing for these two Black men in 1953 was not effortless, particularly because the university's dorms were still new to allowing Black occupants. Rooms were made available near the edge of campus, making the walk to their lab in the brutal weather quite unpleasant. These two Black scientists found their Midwestern hosts to be hospitable, however. Under the Minnesota stars, Brown and Henderson learned the basics of cell and tissue culture and designed their Tuskegee laboratory, preparing for the renovations that would begin when they returned. They needed to be quick studies: Brown stayed in Minnesota for four weeks and Henderson stayed for two. Both were back in Alabama by February 1953.

In April 1953, Scherer headed south to Tuskegee to see the new facility and deliver a precious package. His parcel held contents that were sensitive to temperature swings, and April was one of the few times when Minnesota and Alabama had matching climates. While others on Scherer's airplane drank cocktails (stopping as they flew over dry states), his mind was also on a bottle—the bottle in his carry-on bag. It contained approximately 30 million HeLa cells. When he arrived at the Tuskegee Institute, a liquid was added to those cells, which then fed 40 other bottles. After four days of incubation, each of these bottles contained 30 million more cells, marking the birth of the HeLa cell factory at the Tuskegee Institute.

Inside the Tuskegee HeLa cell factory, cells were grown in a long line of incubators, measured into glass tubes, packaged, and then shipped by air to about two dozen medical laboratories all over the country. Tuskegee's mission was difficult for any school, particularly for a small, underfunded one located in the hot South. HeLa cells died when temperatures broiled around 105 degrees Fahrenheit. While air-conditioning had made the Sunbelt bearable and led to a migration to the South in the 1920s, these sensitive cells were doomed if they traveled in hot cars, waited on hot tarmacs, or sat in hot airplane cargo hulls. So the leadership of the NFIP asked Maria Telkes, a physical chemist at New York University, to come up with a packaging solution to keep the cells cool while in transit. Telkes, an expert on thermal insulation, calculated and designed a special shipping container that resembled a Russian doll. In it, a box covered with insulation sat inside of another box. The inner box contained a can full of the chemical sodium sulfate decahydrate, which rested on top of the glass tubes and kept the cells from overheating. Once placed in these boxes, the cells had to arrive at their destination within 96 hours. One person drove to airports in Montgomery, Ala., and Columbus, Ga., to make sure that these packages did not miss their flights.

There were many failures in getting the HeLa process right and calls and letters from NFIP officials berated Brown about contaminated samples, low cell output, and the arrival of dead cells. Brown, too, was troubled. "The picture at present is distinctly unfavorable," he wrote to the leaders of the NFIP in December 1953. But Norma Gaillard, the cell culture supervisor at Tuskegee, kept making improvements and devised an effective procedure that her technicians followed precisely. The team vigorously hunted down the sources of contamination and installed special air conditioners to keep the lab cool and remove the last vestige of dust and humidity. With time and effort, the technicians eventually exceeded the 10,000 glass tubes of HeLa cells needed to be shipped in a week. By early 1954 the HeLa cell factory was ready to be part of the world's biggest experiment. It was a good thing, too, because summer–and polio season–was coming.

On April 26, 1954, the field trial for Salk's polio vaccine began. This trial was a medical logistics effort on a scale never seen before. The NFIP employed several drug companies to manufacture the vaccine and also mobilized armies of 20,000 doctors, 40,000 nurses, 1,000 public health professionals, 14,000 school principals, 50,000 teachers, and 200,000 volunteers to administer the injections. Overall, nearly 420,000 children were inoculated, and 200,000 were given placebo injections, with an additional 1.2 million other children observed in the study.

Within this huge health campaign was an astronomical number of HeLa cells, which resided inside the 400,000 glass tubes dispatched from a quiet corner of the South. These cells, originating from a Black woman and cultivated by Black scientists, made visible the effectiveness of a long-awaited protection against polio. Ultimately, Thomas Francis Jr., director of the Poliomyelitis Vaccine Evaluation Center at the University of Michigan, announced on April 12, 1955, that the vaccine was "safe, effective, and potent."

The inoculation was approved for distribution, cases of the disease began to drop, and Salk went on to become a national hero. But the role of the Tuskegee Institute and its researchers remained hidden long after the fear of polio faded from the nation's memory.

About the Author

Ainissa Ramirez is a materials scientist and the author of The Alchemy of Us *(MIT Press, 2020). Ramirez writes about little-known contributors to science and has a forthcoming series of children's books about Black inventors (with MIT Kids Press/Candlewick Press).*

Vaccines Reimagined

By Melinda Wenner Moyer

The heat of the sun, a blazing basketball in the West African sky, was softened by a spring breeze one afternoon a few years ago. Every so often the wind whisked a mango off a tree branch and dropped it with a thud on the corrugated iron roof that covered the health center in Bissau, the biggest city in the tiny country of Guinea-Bissau, where the rust-colored ground hadn't felt a raindrop in six months. Inside the building, the air was still and dry, and a line of women and toddlers were sticky with sweat.

An 18-month-old named Maria with thick, dark braids studied me nervously as she perched on her mother's lap. (The child's name has been changed to protect her privacy.) Next to them, Carlito Balé, a soft-spoken doctor in a short-sleeved, white button-down shirt, talked with Maria's mother in Portuguese creole, a percussive fusion of Portuguese and African dialects. Balé was telling the mother that Maria was eligible to participate in a clinical trial to test whether an extra dose of measles vaccine prevented not just the measles but many childhood infections that cause serious illness and death.

In the U.S., where life-threatening infections are rare, such a trial might not garner many volunteers. But in Guinea-Bissau, where lives have been scarred by decades of scant resources and poor medical care, families lined up for it. The nation is one of the world's poorest, and the CIA ranks infant mortality there as the fourth highest among 225 countries. Mothers often wait months to name their babies because one out of every 12 will die before their first birthday.

The researchers leading the trial—anthropologist Peter Aaby and physician Christine Benn, whom I had traveled to Guinea-Bissau to meet—have amassed evidence that a few specific vaccines can thwart a multitude of threatening plagues. Over decades they have published hundreds of studies suggesting that live, attenuated vaccines, which are made from weakened but living viruses or bacteria, can stave off not just their target infections but other diseases, such as respiratory infections (including pneumonia), blood infections (including sepsis), and diarrheal infections. In a 2016 review published in the journal BMJ, a research team commissioned by the World Health Organization analyzed 68 papers on the topic, many of which came from Aaby and Benn's research. It concluded that the measles and tuberculosis vaccines "reduce overall mortality by more than would be expected through their effects on the diseases they prevent." Some of the research the team evaluated linked the measles vaccine with a whopping 50 percent lower risk of death from any cause.

This notion that live vaccines have what are called "off-target" effects–and powerful ones–has implications that stretch far beyond Africa. In 2017 in the U.S., for instance, researchers at the Centers for Disease Control and Prevention reported that children were half as likely to be hospitalized for nonvaccine-targeted infections between the ages of 16 and 24 months if the last immunization they had received was a live vaccine rather than an inactivated one. Recent research in immunology suggests that live vaccines can have such wide-ranging effects because they stimulate a part of the immune system that fights a broad-based war against all outside invaders, giving the system a head start on defense. "Although we still need to know much more about the details, I now have no doubt that vaccines do have some off-target effects because of the support from many different types of evidence," says Frank Shann, a pediatrician at Royal Children's Hospital Melbourne in Australia.

Yet other scientists are far less certain. Aaby and Benn's work is, in fact, quite controversial. For one thing, most of the studies from the two Danish researchers do not prove cause-to-effect connections. "Purported effects" is how Paul Fine, an infectious disease epidemiologist at the London School of Hygiene & Tropical Medicine, describes them. Kids who get live vaccines might survive longer for reasons that have nothing to do with immunizations: the children in those groups might have been healthier to begin with. To address these concerns, Aaby and Benn have been running intervention trials, such as the one Maria was being recruited for.

In it, children will be matched for age and basic health, but some will have only the standard single measles shot at nine months, whereas others will get an additional dose as toddlers.

The two investigators also counter that political and pragmatic concerns drive resistance to their ideas far more than do valid scientific critiques. Aaby says that his and Benn's research is inconvenient for public policy because it indicates that live vaccines should be given last in any vaccine series, which upends current immunization schedules and could inadvertently trigger parental worries about safety. Public health scientists "don't want to hear it, and I can understand why they don't want to hear it," Aaby says. And as a result, he claims, many orthodox vaccine researchers "have clearly made me persona non grata." The 77-year-old, who is bespectacled and has a salt-and-pepper goatee, fits the part of the eccentric, obstinate, and misunderstood scientist so well that he has literally become one in a novel: he inspired a character in a best-selling 2013 Danish mystery book, *The Arc of the Swallow*, who gets murdered in the first chapter.

In real life, Aaby and Benn's ideas may be reaching a tipping point. The WHO wrote in a 2014 report that nonspecific vaccine effects seem "plausible and common" and worthy of more attention. Therefore, in April 2017 the agency announced it would oversee the design of two multiyear clinical trials to further test the hypothesis, although those trials have not yet begun.

The two researchers, whose professional relationship has evolved into a long-term romantic one, are pushing forward with more of their own trials, too. One of them is the study Maria's mother was considering. As I watched in the health center, she decided to enroll her daughter, so Balé picked up a large envelope containing dozens of smaller sealed envelopes and held it open toward her, telling her to pick one–a step that ensured that her daughter would be randomly allocated to either the treatment or control group. Opening her chosen envelope, Balé announced that Maria would get the extra vaccine, and her mother flashed a hopeful smile. She carried her daughter into the next room, where a nurse in a long, white-and-orange tie-dyed dress, black glasses, and a kind smile waited with a needle.

The Measles Clue

In 1979, soon after launching a health surveillance project in Bissau, a young Aaby watched measles kill one out of every four babies in the area. That was the year he saw his first dead body, and he saw a lot more than one.

Back then, childhood vaccines were rare in Africa. The WHO estimates that in 1980, only 6 percent of African children received the first dose of live measles vaccine, and 8 percent got the first inactivated DTP vaccine, which protects against diphtheria, tetanus, and pertussis. It's not as if the vaccine was new; the combination DTP vaccine was licensed in 1949, yet 31 years later fewer than one in 12 African children ever received a dose. Indeed, only a handful of childhood vaccines were even available then in Africa. In addition to the DTP and measles vaccines, there was a live tuberculosis vaccine called bacillus Calmette-Guérin (BCG) and a live polio vaccine. In 1980 in the U.S., on the other hand, 86 percent of kids received the live measles vaccine, 98 percent were inoculated with the inactivated DTP vaccine, and 95 percent had gotten live polio vaccines. African children today receive a lot more vaccines than they used to, but they still woefully lag behind the U.S.

In 1978, a year before the historic measles outbreak began, Aaby had been sent to Guinea-Bissau by a Swedish organization to investigate malnutrition. When the epidemic swept into the city, he pulled strings to import measles vaccines and began to inoculate the local children, all the while keeping track of infection and death rates. The move was a bold one: at that time, public health authorities thought that measles vaccine campaigns in Africa were essentially a waste of money and effort. In a 1981 paper published in the *Lancet*, researchers analyzed survival data after undertaking a measles vaccine campaign in Zaire and concluded that in the future, "it may be useful to think twice before allocating already scarce resources to such a programme." Measles took the lives of the weakest children, they argued; even if the vaccine prevented the infection, the spared children would die from something else soon enough.

Aaby's experience didn't support this argument. The before-and-after numbers he saw were staggering: In 1979, the first year of the outbreak, 13 percent of local children between the ages of six months and three years died; in 1980, when the measles vaccine was available, only 5 percent did. Surprisingly, deaths from causes other than measles dropped by one fifth between 1979 and 1980 too. The trend continued. Even after measles disappeared, immunized children remained more likely than their unvaccinated peers to survive other infections. "It was one of those moments where you can suddenly see something you would never have believed was possible," he recalls. Aaby and his colleagues wrote a letter to the *Lancet* refuting the theory that measles inoculation campaigns in Africa were useless—his first publication in a medical journal. After that, he says of the measles vaccine, "I became obsessed."

Aaby has now published more than 100 studies on this one vaccine. His surveillance program, the Bandim Health Project, a collaboration between Guinea-Bissau's Ministry of Health and the University of Southern Denmark, is one reason why. For more than 40 years the project has been registering all pregnancies, births, and deaths in Bissau's urban district of Bandim, as well as in five nearby rural regions. Aaby's team there has monitored the health of more than 500,000 people living in these areas and has collected data on hospitalizations, vaccinations, and health-related choices, such as whether people sleep with mosquito nets. One day during my visit, as I walked around with Aaby, a mother holding a baby said she remembered him from when he visited her as a child some 30 years ago. His colleagues and assistants in the project affectionately call Aaby "Homem Grande," which translates to "Big Man."

Aaby has always been a bit of a lone wolf—he spends many days working by himself in his home office—but less so during the past 15 years. While Benn was in medical school in 1992 at Aarhus

University in Denmark, she was advised to reach out to Aaby because she wanted to study whether vitamin A supplementation, routinely given with the measles vaccine in developing countries, interacted in any way with the vaccine. "I still have the piece of paper with his number," Benn, who is 53, tells me as she sits on a bench in Aaby's back garden, her arms hugging her legs. She has been working with Aaby ever since. Benn is now a professor of global health at the University of Southern Denmark and runs the Danish arm of the Bandim Health Project. She is prolific, having published more than 200 papers on issues that include the nonspecific effects of vaccines and the impact of vitamin A supplementation on infants in developing countries. She calls Denmark home but spends about 10 weeks a year in Guinea-Bissau. The two researchers bring to the field, and their relationship, complementary personalities: Benn, effervescent, and philosophical; Aaby, serious and precise.

For the most part, Aaby and Benn's work on the measles vaccine has supported Aaby's original observations. In a landmark 1995 BMJ paper, they analyzed data from 12 previously published studies—some their own—on the association between measles vaccination and mortality in developing countries. They found that the vaccine was linked to a 30 to 86 percent reduction in overall death risk. In each study, measles itself killed only a small proportion of unvaccinated kids, so the vaccine wasn't just preventing measles; something else was going on. In a 2014 paper published in *JAMA*, Aaby and Benn collaborated with Danish researchers to investigate whether these protective effects extended to high-income countries. They found that Danish children who received the live measles-mumps-rubella (MMR) vaccine as their last inoculation were 14 percent less likely to be hospitalized for any infection than were kids who had most recently received the inactivated DTaP-IPV-Hib vaccine for diphtheria, tetanus, acellular pertussis, polio, and Hemophilus influenzae type B. This study inspired the 2017 analysis by the CDC that found live vaccines to be associated with even stronger protection in the U.S.

Aaby and Benn have also linked the BCG vaccine with lower neonatal mortality, and they have studied the live oral polio vaccine (OPV) as well. In a 2018 paper, they reported that child mortality rates were 19 percent lower after OPV campaigns than before them, and a clinical trial they published in 2015 found that OPV given within two days of birth with BCG reduced mortality risk by 42 percent, compared with BCG alone. Based in part on their findings, 15 scientists wrote a letter to the *Lancet* in 2016 arguing that the global switch from live OPV to IPV, the inactivated polio vaccine, which is part of a plan developed by the international Global Polio Eradication Initiative, could inadvertently increase child mortality.

The two scientists are certain that the evidence they have accumulated points to a clear conclusion: vaccines have more profound effects on the body than we thought. The big mystery they have been grappling with is how, exactly, all this happens.

A Broad Booster

Mihai G. Netea may have an answer. In 2010, Netea, an immunologist at Radboud University in the Netherlands, embarked on a study that he frankly didn't think would be all that interesting. His laboratory was studying how the BCG vaccine affects human immune cells–how it teaches them to recognize and attack the bacterium *Mycobacterium tuberculosis*. To provide an experimental control on one test, lab workers exposed blood samples from vaccinated volunteers to *Candida albicans*, a common yeast. Based on accepted immunology doctrine, which holds that vaccines incite immune responses specific to the targeted pathogen, BCG should have had no effect on the blood's response to *Candida*.

A few weeks later the student running the test approached Netea, concerned. "I think I did something wrong because I see differences with both tuberculosis and *Candida*," Netea recalls her saying. Perhaps her samples had been contaminated; he suggested that she collect more blood samples and do the experiment over.

She did, but the same thing happened. "She came again and said, 'Well, I don't know what to do, but I see precisely the same thing again,'" Netea says. He was flummoxed, so he started reading about BCG and found a handful of surprising animal studies that suggested the vaccine also protected some animals against malaria, influenza, and *Listeria* monocytogenes, a common cause of foodborne illness.

That is when Netea's simple study transformed into a Greek siren, a creature beckoning for his full attention. How could a vaccine against tuberculosis change how the body responds to other pathogens? The idea contradicted established paradigms. Immunizations prime the body to make proteins called antibodies that recognize, attach to, and attack proteins on the pathogens if the body ever encounters them again. This defense is called adaptive immunity, and it acts like a team of snipers that take out only certain targets. Given adaptive immunity's specificity, it didn't make sense to Netea that it could be responsible for BCG's ability to protect against a number of insults.

Another kind of bodily defense–one that researchers historically thought vaccines had little to do with–is known as innate immunity, and it is more like a battalion told to open fire on anyone who edges into its line of sight. It is the rapid-response team, initiating a fight against any new invader. When pathogens invade, innate inflammatory cells get pulled to the infection site. Large white blood cells called phagocytes–particularly a type called macrophages–engulf and destroy the pathogens. They also secrete immune chemicals called cytokines that draw other immune cells to the scene. The reaction creates proteins that tag pathogens so that they are easier for phagocytes to find.

Given that BCG was increasing protection to multiple pathogens, it made sense to Netea that the innate immune system might be involved. But conventional thinking held that the innate immune system could not "remember" past immunological encounters, such as stimulation from previous vaccines. The thinking has long been that innate immune cells attack whatever they see and then forget about the battle afterward, like a soldier with amnesia. But these assumptions have been woefully incorrect.

In a paper published in 2012 in the *Proceedings of the National Academy of Sciences USA*, Netea's team found that human immune cells primed by BCG produce four times as much of a key cytokine called IFN-gamma (IFN-γ) and twice as much of the cytokines TNF and interleukin-1 beta (IL-1ß) when later exposed to other pathogens. The cells can initiate these enhanced responses for as long as three months after vaccination, which suggests that the innate immune system can, in fact, remember what it learns. More recently, in 2018, the researchers reported that BCG reprograms human immune cells in ways that help them stave off the yellow fever virus.

Netea "has really pioneered a new field within innate immunology," says Helen Goodridge, an immunologist at Cedars-Sinai Medical Center in Los Angeles. Studies by other labs also support Netea's theory, showing that the measles vaccine boosts the body's immune response to the toxin produced by tetanus bacteria, as well as its response when exposed to **Candida**.

It is unclear how the measles vaccine elicits its broad effects, but Netea's work suggests that BCG trains the innate immune system by initiating changes in cellular metabolism and by shaping how key immune genes are controlled. After a person gets BCG, little molecular stamps are placed on important immune-related genes, and these stamps later identify the genes so that they can be quickly turned on when another pathogen invades. Why would a live vaccine elicit these effects better than an inactivated one? Researchers theorize that live organisms may stimulate a different reaction simply because they are alive–not just bits and pieces of an organism, as in the inactivated shots. (Real full-on infections, such as measles, do not seem to produce these advantageous effects and can actually suppress immunity.)

While wrapping up his 2012 study in PNAS, Netea stumbled across a trial that had just been published by Aaby and Benn suggesting BCG reduces general neonatal mortality–a finding that was criticized for being biologically impossible. Excited, Netea wrote to Aaby, telling him he had just discovered a mechanism that made sense of his findings. Since then, the two researchers and Benn have worked together to tease out the immunology behind the Guinea-Bissau data. Vaccines seem to "change the immune system, and they don't just change it in the adaptive, pathogen-specific way," says Tobias Kollmann, an immunologist and infectious disease physician at the University of British Columbia, who sometimes collaborates with Aaby, Benn, and Netea. "They change it in all kinds of different ways."

Trials on Trial

Neal Halsey agrees that Aaby has made important contributions to vaccine research over the course of his career–but says his work on off-target effects is not one of them. Halsey, former director of the Johns Hopkins University's Institute for Vaccine Safety, goes back a long way with the Danish scientist. He remembers that in the 1980s, Aaby was the first to identify a potential safety problem with a new, more concentrated measles vaccine introduced in Guinea-Bissau and other developing countries. At first, no one believed him–this appears to be a recurrent Aaby pattern–but then Halsey looked at data he had collected in Haiti and saw the same effects. Based largely on their findings, the WHO withdrew the vaccine from use in 1992.

But today Halsey thinks that Aaby is putting his convictions before the science. At the 2018 World Vaccine Congress in Washington, D.C., Halsey said the data from Guinea-Bissau may be real, but Aaby and Benn have been drawing causal conclusions from it that they shouldn't. Kids who get vaccinated on time are often quite different from those who don't: they can be healthier to begin with, or they can have wealthier parents with the means to drive them to the doctor and take better care of them in general. Concluding that vaccines are responsible for broadly different medical outcomes is too much of a stretch, Halsey says.

A 2017 BMJ study from the Netherlands illustrates his point. Researchers analyzed hospitalization rates among toddlers who had received a live vaccine as one of their last shots and then compared them with hospitalization rates among toddlers who had most recently gotten only inactivated vaccines. Scientists found that the live-vaccinated kids were 38 percent less likely than the others to be hospitalized for infections–but those children were also 16 percent less likely to be hospitalized for injuries or poisoning. Vaccines should not affect accident risk; the fact that the researchers found this link underscores the notion that vaccine history aligns with other factors in one's life. The authors concede, though, that the way vaccines are administered in the Netherlands–they are scheduled in advance, and parents usually cancel appointments only if their kids are sick–most likely inflates the "healthy vaccinee" effect, as it is called, and findings from other countries may not be skewed so heavily.

Because it is so hard to interpret causality from observational studies, Halsey and others have called for Aaby and Benn to conduct more randomized controlled trials, the so-called gold standard for teasing out an intervention's effects. In these studies, children are randomly selected to receive vaccines or placebos and then followed over time. This random allocation eliminates the chance that socioeconomic status or overall health will play a role in vaccine decisions. The problem is that vaccines are already recommended public policy around the world, so it is unethical for researchers to deny children vaccinations to study them. Thus, scientists must get creative–they have to design trials that provide children with extra vaccines or early ones, or they have to take advantage of natural delays in vaccine receipt.

To undertake a clinical trial in Guinea-Bissau is especially difficult. Aaby and Benn must store vaccines in a refrigerator at their house, where they have a generator, because the electrical grid is so unpredictable (they lost power every day during my visit). Political instability is another problem: one of their attempted trials was disrupted by a devastating civil war in 1998, in which Aaby also suffered a near-fatal wound when he was lanced by a piece of iron left behind by a thief who had looted his house. Some Bissau residents speak only rare dialects, which makes things difficult as well, and many don't have phones.

Despite these challenges, Aaby and Benn are trying randomized trials, such as the one involving Maria. In a few completed tests, the results have not always supported their earlier findings. In a 2018 trial that Aaby and Benn worked on, for instance, researchers found that babies who got the recommended measles vaccine at nine months, plus an additional measles shot between four and 4.5 months, were no less likely to be hospitalized or to die than babies who did not get the extra doses. Yet the two are convinced the vaccine effects are real, just not fully understood. Halsey, though, finds their dogged persistence concerning. "Very good objective scientists acknowledge when an initial observation they made is shown not to be true," he says.

Aaby and Benn are unpopular for another reason: they have published studies suggesting that inactivated vaccines, such as DTP, have detrimental effects, particularly for girls. Even though these vaccines protect against their targeted diseases, Aaby and Benn have linked these shots to a higher risk of other infectious diseases. It is unclear why this would happen–perhaps exposure to dead pathogens makes the immune system more tolerant of other future intruders–and critics argue the associations are not just spurious but also dangerous because they could further undermine the public's confidence in vaccines. "Some of them just think that I'm a madman making trouble," Aaby concedes.

A Search for Clarity

His battles, however, are entering a new phase. Although Aaby notes that his own research funds are running short, the WHO says that it will soon step into the arena. Aaby first contacted the agency about his findings in 1997; in 2013 it established a working group to review the data. In 2014 the WHO noted that the issue deserved further attention, and in 2016 and 2017 it discussed plans to oversee additional trials. One trial will investigate the effects on infant mortality of giving BCG vaccination at birth versus a placebo. The other will evaluate the effects of an extra dose of measles vaccine given with DTP between 12 and 16 months of age.

Aaby and others worry, however, that these trials will yield little clarity. The subjects will be given inactivated vaccines either at the same time as the live vaccines or after them, which, according to Aaby's previous findings, could mute potentially beneficial effects. "We discussed this at length with many experts, and the evidence is clear that those trials will not give the answer," Kollmann observes. Shann, the Australian pediatrician, agrees. These trials will be "a scandalous waste of time and money," he says, because "none of those involved really understands the field." And it is still unclear when the trials will start.

Ultimately Aaby worries that the WHO is just going through the motions. He suspects the agency wants to appear as if it is doing due diligence after its 2014 report on nontargeted effects but that its real goal is to make the issue go away. If nonspecific effects are real and powerful enough to save lives, then public health agencies will have to consider making changes to the vaccine schedule and perhaps even replace some inactivated vaccines with live ones, which would be extremely difficult.

In 2018 I asked Frank DeStefano, director of the CDC's Immunization Safety Office, what it would take to make such changes in the U.S. "Certainly evidence would have to be stronger that this is a real effect," he said. He noted that the agency had no plans at that time to collect more data on the issue. But even if it had additional evidence, he said, the CDC would have to consider all the possible risks and benefits before making policy changes.

Research in the field received renewed attention, however, early on in the COVID-19 pandemic, when scientists at more than 25 universities and clinical centers around the world began trials to test whether certain live vaccines, including the BCG vaccine and the oral polio vaccine, could reduce the risks associated with the coronavirus. Most of the trials are still ongoing.

The evening I left Guinea-Bissau, I sat in the back garden with Benn, eating Danish cheese that she brought with her from her last trip home, and I thought about the couple's philosophy of science. These researchers are not shy about their beliefs; they are convinced that nonspecific effects are real but so complex that many details remain a mystery, and they are not afraid to say so. To critics, this strength of conviction is a great weakness, a blazing preconception that biases their results. And it may do so. But bias is not unique to them. Scientists are people–people with ideas, and prejudices, and feelings–and every study involves interpretation. How do we know whose interpretations edge closest to the truth? Are those who admit to their beliefs more biased than those who don't? Who should decide when enough evidence has amassed to reach a consensus, particularly when the implications are unexpected, inconvenient and consequential? Within this small and contentious field, at least, there are no clear answers.

"You have this feeling you are pulling a thread, and you don't know how big the ball of yarn is," Benn said to me. She was referring to the research on vaccines, but she could have been speaking about the scientific process itself. Biology is immensely complicated because our bodies are complex. The practice of science is complicated, too, because it is a product of humanity–an endeavor created and shaped by our imperfect minds. If vaccines do what Aaby and Benn think they do–and that is still an open question–it will take a lot more messy unraveling before the world sees things their way.

About the Author

Melinda Wenner Moyer, a contributing editor at Scientific American, *is author of* How to Raise Kids Who Aren't Assholes: Science-Based Strategies for Better Parenting–From Tots to Teens *(G. P. Putnam & Sons, 2021).*

Genomic Vaccines Fight Disease in Ways Not Possible Before

By Geoffrey Ling

Standard vaccines to prevent infectious diseases consist of killed or weakened pathogens or proteins from those microorganisms. Vaccines that treat cancer also rely on proteins. In contrast, a new kind of vaccine, which is poised to make major inroads in medicine, consists of genes. Genomic vaccines promise to offer many advantages, including fast manufacture when a virus, such as Zika or Ebola, suddenly becomes more virulent or widespread. They have been decades in the making, but dozens have now entered clinical trials.

Most vaccines work by teaching the immune system to recognize a foe. They accomplish this trick by delivering a dead or weakened pathogen; the immune system recognizes that certain bits of protein, called antigens, on the surface of the pathogen are foreign and prepares to pounce the next time it encounters them. (Many modern vaccines deliver only the antigens, leaving out the pathogens.) To treat cancer, doctors may deliver other proteins that enhance immune responses. These proteins can include the immune system's own guided missiles–antibodies.

Genomic vaccines take the form of DNA or RNA that encodes desired proteins. On injection, the genes enter cells, which then churn out the selected proteins. Compared with manufacturing proteins in cell cultures or eggs, producing the genetic material should be simpler and less expensive. Further, a single vaccine can include the coding sequences for multiple proteins, and it can be changed readily if a pathogen mutates or properties need to be added. Public health experts, for instance, revise the flu vaccine annually, but sometimes the vaccine they choose does not match the viral strains that circulate when flu season comes. In the future, investigators could sequence the genomes of the circulating strains and produce a better-matched vaccine in weeks. Genomics also enables a new twist on a vaccination approach known as passive immune transfer, in which antibodies are delivered instead of antigens. Scientists can now identify people who are resistant to a pathogen, isolate the antibodies that provide that protection and design a gene sequence that will induce a person's cells to produce those antibodies.

With such goals in mind, the U.S. government, academic labs and companies large and small are pursuing the technology. A range of clinical trials to test safety and immunogenicity are under way, including for avian influenza, Ebola, hepatitis C, HIV, and breast, lung, prostate, pancreatic and other cancers. And at least one trial is looking at efficacy: the National Institutes of Health has begun a multisite clinical trial to see if a DNA vaccine can protect against Zika.

Meanwhile researchers are working to improve the technology—for example, by finding more efficient ways to get the genes into cells and by improving the stability of the vaccines in heat. Oral delivery, which would be valuable where medical personnel are scarce, is not likely to be feasible anytime soon, but nasal administration is being studied as an alternative and is under study. Optimism is high that any remaining obstacles can be solved.

About the Author

Geoffrey Ling, a retired U.S. Army colonel, is an expert in technology development and commercial transition. He is a professor of neurology at Johns Hopkins University and the Uniformed Services University of the Health Sciences and a partner of Ling and Associates.

Section 2: Fighting Yourself: Autoimmune Disorders

How I Was Betrayed from Within

By Maria Konnikova

I remember everything about that morning–or as I call it in my mind, in highly scientific terms, the Day That the S*** Totally Hit the Fan. I was getting ready to go to the gym. Usually this was a cause for dread, but that day it was an exciting opportunity to wear the new shorts that had just arrived in the mail. Nothing like shiny new workout gear to get you out and about. I put them on and was about to head out the door when I noticed an intense burning sensation on my thighs. They had become covered, seemingly in seconds, in large, angry hives. I pulled off the new clothes–clearly, something must have gotten on them!–and ran for the shower. Eventually the hives calmed down. Allergic reaction, I assumed, as I returned the shorts to the store in record time. And, I thought, that's that.

My body, it turns out, thought differently. The next morning there they were again. The hives, not the shorts. Only this time they didn't go away. They spread. Within a few days my body was reacting to anything that touched it with mounting anger. It was like some awful internal cascade had been set off, and now nothing could put it back to where it had been before.

This wasn't my first bout with crazed skin reactions. When I was 22, I was diagnosed with mastocytosis. I'd suddenly developed an incredibly painful, oozing J-shaped rash around my left breast. My dermatologist, oddly enough, was overjoyed. Apparently it was rare for the condition (where the body makes too many immune system components called mast cells, which create inflammation) to manifest quite like that in an adult. Fewer than one in 30,000 adults have mastocytosis to begin with, and typically the skin rashes are associated with a childhood onset. After confirming my diagnosis with a painful biopsy, he had asked if he could take photographs for a journal article. I agreed: I was in too much pain to give it much thought, and he just seemed so ... gleeful.

The condition has never gone away for long. When I'm too stressed or tired—or sometimes just hot—a painful raised rash appears. Sometimes it erupts in lesions. It stays for weeks. And then, just like that, it's gone for a year or two or three. The ailment is not an autoimmune disease in itself, but it does mean that my body systematically churns out an abundance of mast cells. Could they be going out of control in my newly developed full-body hives?

It wasn't mastocytosis, my doctor declared at an emergency appointment. My levels of tryptase, an enzyme released by mast cells, were normal. My thyroid, though, was out of whack. Did I have Graves' disease—an autoimmune condition where the immune system attacks the thyroid gland? Or perhaps Hashimoto's, where basically the same thing happens but with the opposite result, too little thyroid hormone to Graves' too much? And if so, where were the hives coming from? Thyroid hormone abnormalities are not connected to hives in most patients.

The world of autoimmune disease is a murky one, often filled with vague guesses. Taken together, autoimmune conditions are common, but many individual illnesses are rare and difficult to diagnose. Oftentimes the diseases strike in infuriatingly hazy ways. Lethargy in the limbs, for instance, could be multiple sclerosis or lupus, devastating but different diseases with a lifetime of debilitating, progressing pain.

A slew of tests followed after my urgent medical visit. They showed my thyroid wasn't to blame. But nothing else was, either. I was shuffled from internists to dermatologists to allergists and immunologists. My sister, a doctor, got me in to see one of the best allergy specialists in the Harvard Medical School system. The result: a host of acronyms I couldn't quite understand, all serving to rule out condition after condition. One of them, the chronic urticaria index, declared that I have "basophil reactive factors in ... serum which supports an autoimmune basis for disease." I asked what that meant. I was told it meant that ... I have hives.

In the absence of answers, the hives continued their colonization of my body. My neck. My face. My eyes, swollen shut. The oral steroid doses increased more and more, along with many antihistamines, which knocked me out to the point where I could barely keep my eyes open. The topical steroid creams got ever stronger. They had huge warnings down the side, urging you to not use them too liberally or for too long, lest your immune system fall apart entirely. I gained weight. I slept too much or not at all. I couldn't think straight for any stretch of time. My immune system was suppressed beyond recognition. And still the cause of the hives remained a mystery. (The shorts, just a coincidence, every specialist assured me, despite my fervent belief in cause and effect.) Idiopathic, read my final diagnosis: origin unknown.

Eventually the hives did recede. Not with any new prescription or diagnosis but with time. The idiopathic hives became rarer hives which became, one glorious morning, a memory. But a memory with no known cause and no real cure. A memory that, to this day, might come back at any moment, with provocation or without. For if you never know what caused it, what's to keep it from recurring?

Autoimmune: "of, relating to, or caused by autoantibodies or T cells that attack molecules, cells, or tissues of the organism producing them." So says the Merriam-Webster dictionary, referring to certain immune system elements. In layperson's terms: attacked by your own body. Instead of your cells uniting against a foreign invader, they turn against one another. Most of the time we don't know what causes it. We don't know how to cure it. When it comes to the autoimmune, the unknowns far outweigh the knowns.

Here's what we know. There are about 80 kinds of autoimmune diseases. Nearly four of every five affected people are women. Why? We're not quite sure. Because here's the other thing we know: autoimmune research is perennially underfunded. Maybe it's because women suffer the most—and women have, historically, been often ignored in medical research. Maybe it's because many conditions are rare. Maybe it's because when a cause is unknown, it is often assumed to be psychosomatic. You make yourself sick. You stress yourself out too much. Are you sure you aren't just making it up?

My sister was thus accused. In her senior year of medical residency, she developed a strange tingling and numbness in her fingertips. For months she ignored it. But the tingling got worse, and the numbness intensified. She went to a neurologist because these could be symptoms of multiple sclerosis. Yet when an MRI test failed to show nerve abnormalities, a doctor said her numbness and pain weren't real. It was all in her head. When she asked for pain medication for what by that point was neuromuscular agony, she was dismissed.

Remember my sister is a physician, with the professional vocabulary to precisely describe what to others would have been hard to capture. And this is what she was met with: disbelief, a medical response familiar to many patients with autoimmune conditions. She pushed back and eventually got a nerve-conduction test. The results were grossly abnormal. She hadn't been lying or pretending. She had CIDP, chronic inflammatory demyelinating polyneuropathy, a rare neurological ailment with autoimmunity features. It causes pain, fatigue, and, in patients like my sister, permanent nerve damage. I can only imagine what would have happened to someone without her medical knowledge and wherewithal.

The world of autoimmune disease is a tough one. It's not just the disbelief. Even with a diagnosis, relief can be elusive. A label is no guarantee of a cure. For CIDP, there is no disease-specific treatment. More than 10 years later my sister is still being treated with a medication developed for MS. Her condition remains understudied and underfunded.

She does have a label, though. I never got one. But here's what I do know. No matter how visible or invisible any given condition, autoimmune disease is incredibly real, incredibly painful–and incredibly underappreciated by those who don't suffer from it. Millions of people are casualties of that lack of awareness.

Here's my wish: that one day I will no longer have to worry whether the next item of clothing I put on will knock me out for another year because someone, somewhere, will have studied what it is that makes me so sick. That one day my sister will be cured.

That one day all the countless sufferers who have been told they're imagining their symptoms are actually listened to—and that when they are, there are tools to help them. Our bodies attack themselves. Let's finally listen. Let's support the research needed to fight back.

About the Author

Maria Konnikova is a science journalist and professional poker player. She is author of the best-selling books The Biggest Bluff *(Penguin Press, 2020),* The Confidence Game *(Viking Press, 2016) and* Mastermind: How to Think Like Sherlock Holmes *(Viking Press, 2013).*

The Terrible Toll of 76 Autoimmune Diseases

By Maddie Bender, Jen Christiansen, Miriam Quick

The idea that organisms might attack themselves with immune systems that evolved to defend them from diseases in the outside world made little sense to immunologist Paul Ehrlich. In 1901 the future Nobel laureate dismissed such a theory—he called it "horror autotoxicus"—as farfetched. Today patients and physicians know that autoimmune diseases are all too real. There are roughly 80 autoimmune conditions that affect millions of people worldwide. The variety and numbers are daunting.

Autoimmunity involves autoantibodies—immune system proteins that mark an organism's own tissues for destruction—along with the T and B cells that serve as agents of that assault. Modern techniques of molecular biology, which have allowed scientists to trace these populations of cells and proteins, have helped refine this definition.

But while the broad outlines are clearer than they were in Ehrlich's day, the details of different illnesses can still be a matter of some dispute. Matthew C. Cook, director of the Center for Personalized Immunology at Australian National University's John Curtin School of Medical Research in Canberra, notes that even in diseases in which scientists do not consistently detect autoantibodies related to pathology, drugs that modulate T cells can be used successfully. The skin illness psoriasis is one such example and is often described as an autoimmune disorder.

Our list includes most of the known diseases in an area where scientific understanding is still evolving. It describes the prevalence of these illnesses, the age at which they typically appear, and whether they are more likely to afflict women or men (almost always women).

There are many autoimmune diseases, and taken together they affect as much as 4.5 percent of the world's population. This list of 76 disorders is drawn from a detailed analysis by immunologists Scott M. Hayter and Matthew C. Cook, then at Australian National University, that was published in 2012. *Scientific American* has updated it with information from other autoimmune disease specialists and the Autoimmune Association (formerly the American Autoimmune Related Diseases Association). The illnesses affect different parts of the body, and several strike multiple organs. Women are most frequently afflicted, although the exact gender ratios differ among individual diseases. The approximate average ages of onset and the frequency in the population also vary.

Immunologists and rheumatologists acknowledge that autoimmunity can be a murky research area, and they are still discovering features that characterize a disorder as autoimmune or not. In general, the diseases presented here fall into three categories, based on the strength of evidence that they are driven by an autoimmune response and proteins known as autoantibodies. In the clearest cases, such as Graves' disease, the illness definitely involves autoantibodies that lead to an immune system assault, inflammation, and debilitating symptoms. In many others, including Guillain-Barr syndrome, autoantibodies are often present, but scientists have not been able to tie them consistently to the pathology of the disease. Finally, some disorders do not always show autoantibodies, yet they respond well to treatments that affect the immune system. This response suggests the illnesses have an autoimmune component. Ulcerative colitis and psoriasis are two examples in this group.

Some conditions that have autoantibodies and appear to be related to autoimmunity have been excluded from this list. That is because they were not part of Cook and Hayter's survey, or they were not on a compendium from the Autoimmune Association, or some autoimmune disease specialists contend that certain biological features made their status debatable. These ailments include myocarditis, neuromyelitis optica, primary membranous nephropathy, and thrombotic thrombocytopenic purpura.

About the Authors

Maddie Bender is a science writer and podcaster based in Boston, Mass.

Jen Christiansen is senior graphics editor at Scientific American.

Miriam Quick is a data journalist and researcher specializing in information visualization.

Targeted Treatments for Autoimmune Disease Make Progress

By Marla Broadfoot

When Magdalene Quintero was 14 years old, her mouth filled with painful ulcers that made eating and drinking unbearable. Her normally tawny skin flamed crimson red across the bridge of her nose and cheeks. The tips of her fingers burst into open sores, as if she had dipped them in acid. She spiked fevers, developed headaches, lost weight, and was always tired.

It took a year of visits to various doctors for Quintero to learn that she had lupus, a life-threatening and chronic autoimmune condition that can cause pain, inflammation, and damage to any part of the body. It took another two years for her rheumatologist–the only one at the Indian Health Service serving her community of Jones, Okla.–to find medications in the right doses to bring her disease under control.

Quintero, who is now 25, considers herself lucky. Lupus also struck her younger sister, Isabel Hernandez, and has taken a more terrifying form. It began with constant nosebleeds. By the time Isabel was diagnosed, at age 17, her lungs were hemorrhaging blood. She spent 88 days on a ventilator before relearning how to walk, talk, and eat. Today, at age 21, her kidneys are failing. Every day she spends hours having her blood filtered by a dialysis machine, waiting for a transplant.

"It is so heartbreaking," says Quintero, who recently completed her master's degree in biomedical science at Oklahoma State University. She worries whether her future holds a similar fate. "But I also feel thankful for my own health and fortunate that the medications that I'm on are doing their job," she says.

Lupus has been called "the great imitator" because its symptoms–including fever, fatigue, joint pain, rashes, headaches, memory problems, and organ failure–often mimic many other autoimmune conditions. Those symptoms reveal the many ways our bodies can turn against us as a wayward immune system, intended to defend us, attacks our own healthy cells.

Traditionally therapies for lupus and other autoimmune diseases have relied on decades-old blunt-force strategies that essentially bludgeon a badly behaving immune system into submission. But these approaches cause collateral damage that sometimes can be worse than the disease itself. Foremost among these treatments are steroids, medications that have unparalleled ability to dampen the entire immune response but in doing so can leave patients vulnerable to dangerous and even deadly infections.

Recent research is fueling a shift in the way autoimmune diseases are treated, based on a more nuanced approach. Distributed throughout the body, the human immune system is a dizzyingly complex network of many different types of cells, organs, tissues, and proteins, which communicate with one another through a wide variety of chemical messages. Modern technology, such as gene assays and molecular engineering, is enabling scientists to target individual parts of this network, identifying new targets for treating autoimmunity with much more precision. Some of these new therapies aim to interfere with autoantibodies, rogue antibodies that take aim at healthy cells. Others work by hobbling key chemical messengers that are passed among immune cells.

But these treatments do not work for all patients, and many diseases prove stubbornly resistant, which is why many people with autoimmune problems are drawn to approaches outside of mainstream medicine. Among scientists, the successes and failures are creating a new appreciation for the precarious balance our body maintains between protection and pathology. Half of the immune system—such as cytotoxic or "killer" T cells and antibody-producing B cells—is designed to fight. The other half—mainly regulatory T cells—is designed to keep the peace. When the former goes rogue and the latter fails to keep it in check, autoimmune disease ensues. "All of us, every one of us, has the potential to develop autoimmunity," says V. Michael Holers, a rheumatologist at the University of Colorado

School of Medicine, "because our immune system develops with this kind of yin and yang."

Early Warnings

For decades steroids such as prednisone and dexamethasone have been the mainstay of treatment for patients with autoimmune conditions. These potent anti-inflammatory drugs indiscriminately shut down the production of cytokines, the key messengers that rouse our vast army of immune cells to fight a perceived threat. Although steroids can be extremely effective at reducing the signs and symptoms of autoimmunity, they exact a price so high that some people liken it to making a deal with the devil. Many patients are stuck taking these medications, orally or by injection, for much of their lives. And steroids can create a whole host of other problems, such as cataracts, mood swings, weight gain, trouble sleeping, thinning bones, high blood pressure, high blood glucose, and increased risk of infection.

Furthering the problem is that by the time most patients with autoimmune diseases seek treatment, a lot of damage is already done. Autoantibodies have been stealthily coursing through the blood and tissues for months or years, leading to ongoing assaults on a targeted organ—pancreas, kidneys, joints, gut, skin, hair follicles, brain, spinal cord. As a result, treatments such as steroids are defensive in nature, focused on keeping the disease from getting worse or damping down flare-ups.

Now there is a big push among physician-scientists to go on the offense, correcting autoimmune imbalances before they produce their most devastating consequences. Researchers hope focusing on early treatment and prevention could lower the burden of autoimmune disease, much as treating people at high risk of cardiovascular disease with blood pressure medications and cholesterol-lowering drugs has reduced the prevalence of heart attacks and strokes. Several trials investigating this idea are underway for type 1 diabetes, rheumatoid arthritis, lupus, and multiple sclerosis.

There are already some early successes. In one study, researchers recruited 76 people with a family history of type 1 diabetes, who also had abnormal blood sugar levels and at least two diabetes-related autoantibodies. Half the participants received an experimental drug, a monoclonal antibody called teplizumab that interferes with the immune system assault on insulin-producing beta cells in the pancreas. The other half received a placebo. More than five years later only 50 percent of people treated with a two-week course of the drug had developed the disease, compared with 78 percent of those who received a placebo. The researchers estimate that in those who did develop the disease, early treatment delayed onset by nearly three years.

"That's a big deal," says endocrinologist Carla Greenbaum, director of the TrialNet Hub, which coordinates the clinical trial network leading the study and others like it. "This is a disease that affects every moment of every day of your life, so any time without it is clinically important." By fine-tuning this approach, scientists hope they can extend the disease-free period and perhaps discover ways to block the destruction entirely. And Greenbaum thinks the idea should work for other ailments. "We are really the template for all these other autoimmune diseases that are now also discovering these long preclinical periods," she says.

Multiple sclerosis (MS) is another autoimmune condition where early detection is crucial. It affects the central nervous system, and a telltale sign is white matter lesions, spots on the brain and spinal cord where the disease has stripped the protective covering off the nerves. Over the past decade researchers have found these abnormalities in hundreds of people with no outward symptoms of MS, who came to their notice only after an unrelated concussion or migraine landed them in a brain-scanning machine. David Hafler, a neurologist at the Yale School of Medicine, believes these cases, known as radiologically isolated syndrome (RIS), could represent the earliest-known stage of MS. He and his colleagues have launched a multicenter study with biotech firm Genentech to treat RIS with ocrelizumab, a drug commonly used to treat later stages of MS.

And Hafler would like to find other biological hallmarks that would allow intervention even before the lesions appear. "The ultimate treatment for autoimmunity is to identify [people who are at high risk] and treat them before the disease really begins," he says.

Sharpening the Target

Drugs such as monoclonal antibodies offer the important advantage of being able to go after specific immune system elements that cause a given disease while–unlike steroids–leaving the rest of the immune system functional. But this new targeted approach comes with its share of difficulties. Although it has expanded the therapeutic options for patients, it has also fizzled or even backfired in some cases, making patients worse. Harmony within the immune system, it turns out, is not easy to achieve.

Several targeted therapies focus on a particularly powerful cytokine called tumor necrosis factor, or TNF. It goes haywire in many autoimmune diseases, setting off waves of damaging inflammation. Monoclonal antibody drugs that block its action are widely used in the treatment of rheumatoid arthritis, inflammatory bowel disease, and psoriasis. Yet clinical trials in multiple sclerosis showed that TNF inhibitors actually exacerbate the disease. "It is one of the great curiosities of autoimmunity," Hafler says. What's more, targeted therapies that suppress autoimmune disease in one patient have been shown to trigger that same disease in other patients.

Belimumab, one of only three new medications approved for lupus in the past 60 years, also is a targeted therapy. It blocks a cytokine called B lymphocyte stimulator, or BLyS (pronounced "bliss"), that keeps autoreactive B cells going, extending an autoimmune reaction. Although the treatment has helped many patients, a significant number of them get no benefit, suggesting that different molecular mechanisms may be at play in different people, according to Judith James, a rheumatologist at the Oklahoma Medical Research Foundation.

Luckily, technological advances are enabling researchers to dissect differences–among patients and between diseases–at the genetic level, illuminating patterns that could explain past failures and point the way to future successes. For example, attempts to treat alopecia areata, an autoimmune assault on hair follicles that causes large clumps of hair to fall out, have typically repurposed drugs from the seemingly related skin conditions psoriasis and atopic dermatitis. None of them have worked. When Angela Christiano, a geneticist at Columbia University who has alopecia, completed a study on the genetic basis of the disorder, she suddenly realized why. “You can read it like a road map,” she says. “There’s a reason they failed: we don’t share any genetic pathways with either of those two diseases.” Christiano has learned the illness has more in common with rheumatoid arthritis, celiac disease, and type 1 diabetes than it does with skin ailments. “I think it is a great example of how genetics can completely realign your thinking,” Christiano says.

One of the genes she identified, ULBP3, acts as a distress signal that damaged cells use to tell killer T cells to take them out. Normally the gene turns on only if a cell is cancerous, infected, or dying. But in hair follicles affected by alopecia, the gene is stuck in the on position, constantly signaling for the cells’ own demise. That signal involves the production of a type of cytokine called a Janus kinase, or JAK. Christiano showed that a class of drugs known as JAK inhibitors, often used to disrupt autoimmune signaling in rheumatoid arthritis, could thwart the killer T cells’ attack on hair follicles. Within a few months of treatment, patients who were once bald regrew full heads of hair. When Christiano was diagnosed with alopecia early in her career, no one could tell her whether she would get better or worse, and the only treatments available involved injecting steroids into her scalp. Now her work has led to multiple advanced trials of JAK inhibitors for the illness.

Six JAK inhibitors are already approved for other autoimmune and inflammatory diseases, and numerous others are in the pipeline.

Still, there are no guaranteed breakthroughs, and even the latest targeted treatments could have off-target effects. For example, in February 2021 the U.S. Food and Drug Administration warned of an increased risk of heart-related problems and cancer associated with a JAK inhibitor being used to treat rheumatoid arthritis.

"That's the reality of autoimmune disease therapy right now, so I always say it's worth searching for the lesser of all the evils," says Aimee Payne, a dermatologist at the University of Pennsylvania who is developing gene therapy for a rare autoimmune skin disorder called pemphigus vulgaris. People with this disease have autoantibodies that attack a protein called desmoglein-3 (DSG3), which normally glues skin cells together. When that protein is destroyed, it causes painful blisters to form all over the body, sometimes sending patients into burn units to be treated for life-threatening infections.

For Magdalene Quintero and her sister, their lives feel shaped by their illnesses. Her sister takes 19 medications to manage her lupus symptoms.

Payne has devised a targeted treatment, tested in mice, that could eliminate the specific population of B cells producing these autoantibodies but leave other B cells alone. The immune system has billions of B cells, which come in many different kinds. The vast majority of them produce antibodies needed to fight viruses and bacteria. Fortunately, the anti-DSG3 B cells are easy to find because they have a highly distinctive marker—basically a version of the anti-DSG3 autoantibody stuck on their surfaces. "In some ways, these B cells are terrible criminals because they're declaring what they're going to attack before they ever attack it," Payne says.

To get rid of these disease-causing cells, Payne used a technique invented by her colleague Michael Milone that has successfully eliminated malignant B cells in certain blood cancers. The strategy, called CAR T cell therapy, uses genetically engineered killer T cells that have a kind of homing beacon known as a chimeric antigen receptor (CAR). It steers the T cells to other specific cell types in a search-and-destroy mission. In adapting the technique to treat autoimmune disease, the team gave T cells a beacon derived from bits of the anti-DSG3 autoantibody, which leads the killers straight to anti-DSG3 B cells.

When the researchers infused the engineered T cells into a mouse model of pemphigus vulgaris, the blisters disappeared. Payne founded a biotech start-up to move the treatment forward to clinical trials, which are currently ongoing. Because the treatment is made of living cells that can replicate and remember their target, she thinks a single infusion could last decades. "My dream is the one-and-done," she says. "A precision cure of disease."

Other researchers are using a related technique to tip the balance on the other side of the autoimmunity equation. Rather than mobilizing killer T cells, they are amplifying the calming power of regulatory T cells to suppress the overactive immune system. Still in early stages, the approach has shown promise in animal models of ulcerative colitis, multiple sclerosis, and rheumatoid arthritis.

Beyond Drugs

Although pharmaceuticals make up the bulk of the growing armamentarium against autoimmune diseases, some of the most intriguing additions explore alternative ways to restore balance in the body.

Many of our basic bodily functions–heart rate, blood pressure, digestion, respiratory rate, and sexual arousal–are governed by two opposing forces. The sympathetic nervous system initiates the energetic "fight or flight" response, whereas the parasympathetic nervous system halts this activity and prepares the body to "rest and digest." Our ability to shift from one state to the other depends largely on the vagus nerve, a bundle of 100,000 nerve fibers that runs from the brain stem down to the diaphragm before shooting out its tendrils to the heart, gut, and other organs. Some research suggests this influential piece of anatomy starts to malfunction before people develop autoimmune diseases. "It would be like the brake failing on your car when you are going down the mountain," says Kevin Tracey, a neurosurgeon at the Feinstein Institutes for Medical Research, based in Manhasset, N.Y.

Tracey has shown that stimulating the vagus nerve with tiny jolts of electricity can reset the nervous system and actually helps to calm overactive immune cells. He and other researchers have traced the way signals from a small electrical device implanted in the neck travel down the vagus nerve all the way to the spleen, where they shut down the production of TNF and other inflammatory molecules. Initial clinical trials suggest a small zap to the vagus nerve could reduce the severity of rheumatoid arthritis and Crohn's disease, even when delivered through a less invasive device that stimulates a branch of the vagus near the ear when it is pressed against the skin. A company Tracey co-founded recently launched a multicenter randomized, controlled trial of the implantable stimulator. (Similar vagus nerve stimulators are already approved by the FDA for treating epilepsy and depression.)

Another unconventional method looks to correct immune system imbalance with a decidedly lower-tech intervention: fecal transplants. The idea of transplanting fecal matter from one person to another originated in ancient Chinese medicine, when a stool slurry called "yellow soup" was used to treat severe food poisoning and diarrhea. In modern times, fecal transplants have become an accepted therapy for a dangerous gut infection caused by *Clostridium difficile*, or *C. diff*.

A few years ago gastroenterologist Jessica Allegretti and other researchers noticed that in patients with *C. diff* problems, a fecal transplant not only resolved the infection but also helped concurrent cases of inflammatory bowel disease (IBD). The severe digestive distress of IBD stems from inflammation, and some scientists think an autoimmune reaction is involved, although the notion is a matter of some debate. Still, the results "got the community excited about this potential," says Allegretti, who directs the fecal microbiota transplant program at Brigham and Women's Hospital in Boston. Plus, the finding makes sense. There are distinct differences in the populations of gut microorganisms–known as the microbiome—between nonaffected people and those with ulcerative colitis, a subtype of IBD that does appear to involve autoimmunity. These changes most likely reflect an imbalanced state where pro-inflammatory microbes dominate over anti-inflammatory ones.

Four randomized clinical trials have tested fecal transplants in ulcerative colitis. In all, about a third of patients went into remission, rates similar to those seen with immunosuppressive medications. More studies and clinical trials of the transplants are underway for rheumatoid arthritis, lupus, multiple sclerosis, and alopecia areata, further testing the limits of this odd healing modality.

Out of the Mainstream

Fecal transplants are not FDA-approved for any medical condition, so don't expect them to emerge as autoimmune treatments anytime soon. Allegretti says the slow track is the right one. "I think there's a misconception that because this is 'natural' it is somehow safer than regular drugs, and I don't think that's true at all," she says. "We are only just starting to understand the long-term consequences of these therapies, and I think they deserve the respect of being studied appropriately in the way we study all drugs." The scientific literature is littered with accounts of home fecal transplants gone wrong, such as the case of a man with ulcerative colitis who attempted the procedure with stool from his infant son and his wife and landed in the hospital with a cytomegalovirus infection.

Yet many people with autoimmune disorders, frustrated with the lack of conventional therapies and impatient with doctors who offer little help and less hope, are willing to take their health into their own hands, using approaches within and outside mainstream medicine to manage their autoimmune symptoms. Joe Person, for instance, is a 37-year-old based in Washington, D.C., who has lupus. When he was diagnosed in his senior year of college, he drafted a decision tree of the possible tests, complications, outcomes, and medications. At his first appointment with his rheumatologist, he demanded to be put on the antimalarial drug hydroxychloroquine, which has helped ease lupus symptoms and is the basis of early treatment and prevention trials.

Fifteen years later Person credits that early action with keeping the illness at bay, although he does have physical fatigue and feels his brain works slowly at times. “The takeaway I’ve gotten from rheumatologists is just sit there and wait for us to invent the pharmaceutical that works,” Person says. “Unfortunately, sitting around and doing nothing is antithetical to every survival instinct in my body. I want to do as much as I can proactively, if nothing else to just feel like I’m exploring all options to stay ahead of this.” He went into remission after switching to a raw vegan diet, only to have his disease flare when he developed an allergy to raw vegetables. And he installed a tanning bed in his basement to test out a theory that certain wavelengths of ultraviolet light can relieve lupus symptoms, although he has yet to see any positive results.

Some scientists are open to alternatives. Tracey says strategies such as acupuncture could, in theory, reduce stress and inflammation by activating certain branches of the nervous system, although he adds that such approaches sometimes make it “hard to prove cause and effect.” To stimulate a healthy gut microbiome without an illegal stool infusion, Allegretti recommends trying fiber-rich foods and plant-based diets. And James advises people with autoimmune problems to avoid smoking and get plenty of sleep, which help the body reduce inflammation: basically “all those things your mother told you,” she says.

For Magdalene Quintero and her sister, their lives feel shaped by their illnesses. Her sister takes as many as 19 medications to manage her lupus symptoms. Quintero needs to take only two drugs right now and has spent the past few years working under the mentorship of James at the Oklahoma medical foundation, first in the lab and now in the clinic, trying to improve treatments for the disease. She remembers how her great aunt, who also had lupus, spent the last years of her life in a wheelchair, her bones ravaged by steroids. “Back then they didn’t have the treatments we have,” she says. Quintero is now trying to get into a medical school or a physician assistant program, determined to put herself in a position to alter the course of the disease that has tormented her family.

About the Author

Marla Broadfoot is a freelance science writer who lives in Wendell, N.C. She has a Ph.D. in genetics and molecular biology.

How Blood Sugar Can Trigger a Deadly Immune Response in the Flu and Possibly COVID-19

By Tanya Lewis

Many of the people dying in the novel coronavirus pandemic appear to be harmed more by their own immune system than by the virus itself. The infection can trigger a cytokine storm–a surge in cell-signaling proteins that prompt inflammation–that hits the lungs, attacking tissues and potentially resulting in organ failure and death. But this phenomenon is not unique to COVID-19; it sometimes occurs in severe influenza too. Now a study sheds light on one of the metabolic mechanisms that help orchestrate such runaway inflammation.

Scientists have long known that viral infections can affect human cellular metabolism, the system of biochemical reactions needed to provide energy for everything cells do. In the new paper, researchers showed that in live mice and human cells, infection with an influenza A virus–one of two types that typically cause seasonal flu–sets off a chain of cellular events, or a pathway, that boosts the metabolism of glucose. This action, in turn, triggers the production of an avalanche of cytokines. And blocking a key enzyme involved in the glucose pathway could be one way to prevent a deadly cytokine storm, according to the study, which was published last week in Science Advances.

Although the research was not focused on the novel coronavirus, the team says the same mechanism is likely at play in the illness it causes: COVID-19. This connection could explain why people with diabetes are at a higher risk of dying from the virus.

When a virus infects a cell, it steals resources in order to make copies of itself, explains Paul Thomas, an immunologist at St. Jude Children's Research Hospital in Memphis, Tenn., who was not involved in the new study. Infected cells have to boost their metabolism to replenish these resources, and healthy cells must also do so in order to mount an effective immune response, he says.

Prior research had shown that an influenza infection increases the metabolism of glucose, the sugar molecule that fuels most cellular activities. And in previous work, the authors of the new paper had identified a pathway, involving a signaling protein called interferon regulatory factor 5 (IRF5), in which a flu infection can lead to a cytokine storm.

In its latest study, the team revealed, at a detailed molecular level, how a glucose metabolism pathway activated by flu infection leads to an out-of-control immune response. During such an infection, high levels of glucose in the blood cause an enzyme called O-linked -N-acetylglucosamine transferase (OGT) to bind to, and chemically modify, IRF5 in a process known as glycosylation. This step enables another chemical modification, called ubiquitination, that leads to a cytokine inflammatory response.

The researchers infected mice with influenza A and then administered glucosamine, a sugar that kicks off this glucose metabolism pathway. They showed that doing so increased the production of cytokines. Next, they genetically engineered mice that lacked the gene that enables OGT production. These mice did not develop an over-the-top cytokine response when exposed to glucosamine.

Finally, the scientists analyzed blood collected from flu patients and healthy individuals in Wuhan, China, between 2018 and 2019. They found that the flu-infected subjects' blood had higher glucose levels–and correspondingly higher levels of immune system signaling molecules–than that of the healthy patients. That result further supports the idea that glucose metabolism plays a role in flu infection.

The findings suggest that interfering with this pathway could be one way to prevent the cytokine storm seen in flu and other viral infections. Such an intervention would need to be done carefully, however, to avoid shutting off the body's ability to fight the virus altogether.

"It could be relevant to interfere with glucose metabolism using chemical inhibitors and [to] modulate the cytokine production," says study co-author Mengji Lu, a professor at University Hospital Essen's Institute of Virology in Germany. "But it needs to be said that energy metabolism is essential for our immune cells [to fight a] virus. It may be important to combine antiviral treatment and metabolic inhibitors–suppressing the virus and reducing the overshooting immune reaction at the same time."

A similar process of runaway cytokine production has been observed in COVID-19, Lu says. But there are no specific drugs that target the SARS-CoV-2 virus that causes the disease, he adds, so "interference with energy metabolism alone may result in breakdown of our immune defense and does not provide a benefit."

Other researchers praise the study. "This paper does a nice job of proposing and validating one mechanism by which metabolic changes can feed forward to inflammatory responses," Thomas says. Previous studies had shown more broadly that glucose metabolism plays a role in the response to flu infection. But this one details what is going on at the molecular level and how interfering with this process could prevent uncontrolled inflammation, he adds.

The findings confirm what Haitao Wen, now an assistant professor of immunology at Ohio State University, and his colleagues found in a 2018 study of the same metabolic pathway using a different RNA virus. A 2019 study by another group also came to similar conclusions. All three studies show that the OGT enzyme involved in this pathway is required to initiate the host's stress response to a viral infection. "The initial point of this stress response is to build up an antipathogen immune response and try to fight against virus," says Wen, who was not involved in the new paper. "But if the inflammatory response keeps going, it will cause collateral damage."

Given the role of glucose in the pathway, could a person's diet have an effect on their response to a viral infection? "That's a very good question," Wen says. "At this moment, I think it's too early to make a judgment [about whether] a special diet can fight against virus infection." What scientists do know is that people with type

2 diabetes are more susceptible to severe flu infections. But that risk is not because they have higher glucose levels in their blood. The real reason, Wen says, is that they cannot use glucose effectively–and thus cannot initiate a proper antiviral response.

Ultimately, the hope is that by interfering with this glucose metabolism pathway, we might be able to stave off the deadly cytokine storms seen in severe cases of flu or COVID-19. But Lu's team has not yet done studies in people. "At the moment, we do not have data in patients demonstrating the effect of interference with energy metabolism," he says. "It is too early to make a conclusion about the potential clinical use."

About the Author

Tanya Lewis is a senior editor at Scientific American *who covers health and medicine.*

How to Kill HIV: Target Its "Influencers"

By Apoorva Mandavilli

In just about any system or group, elements with a larger number of connections tend to have more clout than others. Think of Instagram "influencers," for example—or the chief executive officers of companies.

Even within a virus, some structural components—in this case, parts of proteins—have more links to one another than others do. And coaching the immune system to recognize and destroy such influencers is an efficient way to kill HIV, suggests a study published in May 2019 in *Science*.

There has been a lot of excitement in the HIV field since the March 2019 announcement that a second person, often referred to as the "London patient," was cured after a bone marrow transplant. The donor carried a mutation that makes people naturally resistant to HIV; in effect, the procedure replaced the patient's immune system with a new, resistant one. But bone marrow transplants are risky and invasive, and many experts believe a practical cure for the nearly 38 million HIV-infected people worldwide is more likely to come from smart molecular work. Most research done on HIV cures has so far focused on buttressing a person's immune system. The *Science* study turns that approach on its head by looking for the most critical parts of the virus itself.

For this study, the researchers focused on "elite controllers"—people whose bodies control the virus without the aid of any drugs and who are estimated to number about one in every 300 infected individuals. It made sense that investigating how their immune systems kill HIV might point the way to a cure, says Bruce Walker, who is senior author of the paper and director of the Ragon Institute of Massachusetts General Hospital, the Massachusetts Institute of Technology, and Harvard University. "There are not two people who are cured of HIV infection, in my view," Walker says. "There are thousands–and a lot of them who control [the virus] on their own. We, as a field, need to pursue this with the highest priority."

Walker and his colleagues found that elite controllers' immune systems target the most influential regions in the virus. The researchers made this discovery by applying network theory, a type of analysis frequently used in mathematics to chart relationships between objects. They employed the theory to map connections between amino acids, the building blocks of proteins, in three-dimensional molecular structures of HIV proteins. (They used the 3-D structures because two amino acids that appear far apart in a protein's linear sequence may be much closer–and connected–in three dimensions.)

The researchers found that some amino acids tend to have numerous branchlike structures that cause them to interact with many other amino acids. These branched amino acids have a high "network score," Walker says, and are thus the most important to HIV's integrity. HIV can mutate in a defensive response to a drug that targets a specific part of its structure. But the amino acids with high network scores are so important that the virus cannot vary them without great cost to itself: if those amino acids change, the connections are lost.

"If you take a highly networked [amino acid] and mutate it, the virus basically falls apart," Walker says. "It dramatically loses fitness." This finding makes such amino acids attractive targets for therapy because attacking them puts the virus in a lose-lose situation: it ends up destroyed whether it mutates or not. Walker's team found that elite controllers' immune systems tend to selectively target these influencer amino acids; in most other infected people, immune systems instead mount futile attacks on other, less important parts of the virus.

"This is impressive and important work,"comments Andrew McMichael, an emeritus professor of molecular medicine at the University of Oxford, who cowrote a commentary accompanying the paper but was not involved in the research. "It explores why some [immune responses] are effective and why some are less effective."

The research may also resolve some previously inconsistent findings about an immune molecule called B*57–which has been suggested as a magic weapon that elite controllers wield against HIV. B*57 is part of a group of molecules called human leukocyte antigens (HLAs), which make up a key part of the immune system. HLAs carry fragments of viruses to an infected cell's surface so that killer immune cells circulating in the blood can recognize the flagged cell as infected and destroy both that cell and the virus within it.

There are thousands of HLA types, some more common than others, and some are better at controlling certain infections. Among these, B*57 is thought to be particularly potent against HIV. But scientists have been puzzled by the fact that not everyone with B*57 is an elite controller–nor do all elite controllers carry B*57. The new research suggests that what is key is not so much B*57 itself but the influencer amino acids that it targets.

B*57 "is the major determinant of progression or nonprogression [of HIV infection], but it's not totally flawless," McMichael says, adding that the 2019 paper "goes some way toward explaining why that may be."

Walker and others have studied elite controllers for decades. One such person, Loreen Willenberg, now 67 years old, was diagnosed in 1992 and has since donated hundreds of samples for research. Willenberg, who says she has "an amazing immune system," is invulnerable to dozens of pathogens, including HIV. Tests that measure her immune response to HIV still come back positive, but no test can detect the virus itself. "I've never measured a viral load, ever. It's always been undetectable," Willenberg says.

Walker had been following Willenberg's health for about 15 years at the time of the study. But this time, instead of focusing on the aspects of her genetics that protect her from HIV, the team homed in on which parts of HIV her system attacks. "Here we don't take into account host genetics at all," Walker says. Yet the study still explains what makes her immune system so remarkable: it selectively attacks the amino acids with the highest network scores. "She fit the pattern perfectly," he says.

With this confirmation of the importance of these influential amino acids, Walker says he hopes to develop a "therapeutic vaccine" that can be given to people already infected with HIV. The vaccine would contain about 30 of the viral parts with the highest network scores. The hope is that it would prime an infected person's immune system to recognize and then go after these key targets and destroy the virus.

"We believe we can redirect the immune response," Walker says. "We don't know whether this will work, but there is a very strong rationale for it to do so."

About the Author

Apoorva Mandavilli is a reporter for the New York Times, *focusing on science and global health. Her work has been published in the* Atlantic, Slate *and the* New Yorker *online.*

Section 3: Hacking a Cure for Cancer and Other Diseases

A Shot against Cancer

By Beatriz M. Carreno, Elaine R. Mardis

For more than a decade researchers have been trying to supercharge human defense systems against cancer with the help of a vaccine. These injections are not designed to prevent cancer from starting. Instead they provide patients' immune system with intel on what the enemy—cancer cells—looks like. Ordinarily, cancerous cells do not look different enough from normal cells to trigger an immune system response, but we have figured out ways to highlight and target some of the proteins that are unique to these malignancies.

Human cells are covered in so-called self-proteins that serve as identifying markers for the immune system. Like an ID card, they let the body know whether a substance belongs in the body and should not be attacked. Unfortunately, those proteins also dot the exterior of cancerous cells. Earlier cancer vaccine efforts, by our team and others, may have failed because they primed the immune system to look for proteins present—though at different levels—on both.

Recently, however, our team has managed to home in on proteins that are unique to the malignancies by scouring genome sequences of a patient's normal tissue and a tumor to identify proteins exclusive to the cancer. Then we study which cancer-specific proteins spark a strong response from immune molecules charged with directing the body's response to foreign substances, called major histocompatibility complex proteins, or MHCs. Using that information, we can create personalized vaccines that include MHC-containing dendritic cells from the patient that will grab the cancer proteins and present them to the immune system. That stimulus helps to generate antitumor T cell responses and marks cancer cells bearing those specific proteins for destruction.

Last year we tried this approach with three melanoma patients. As we wrote in Science, we found seven cancer-specific proteins that would bind to each patient's MHC molecules. We were thrilled to see a response in all three subjects: three of the seven proteins were recognized by the patients' T cells, and those T cells attacked the patients' cancer cells.

A year later the patients' immune system continued producing antitumor T cells in the blood, suggesting that our vaccines could fight off tumor recurrences. (Two of our patients' tumors shrunk or stabilized, but because they received other therapies, too, we do not know what helped.) To date, all three patients are alive and stable and show no negative side effects from the vaccine.

Our work is still in its early days. We first selected melanoma to treat because it is a cancer with many mutations and protein targets, but we plan to test this approach with other cancers too. Before our method could become part of routine cancer therapy, we would need to study how it affects tumors long term and speed up our vaccine production time. Eventually we would like to use these vaccines to complement other cancer immunotherapies. Ultimately, we hope, vaccines will give patients a better shot against cancer.

About the Authors

Beatriz M. Carreno is an associate professor of medicine at Washington University in St. Louis. She studies how human immunology and cancer genomics may improve therapies directed at cancer.

Elaine R. Mardis is Robert E. and Louise F. Dunn Distinguished Professor of Medicine and co-director of the McDonnell Genome Institute at Washington University in St. Louis. She studies how human immunology and cancer genomics may improve therapies directed at cancer.

Are We Innately Immune to Cancer?

By Mark Lowdell

The study of cancer immunity has been a global challenge since William Coley first treated patients with his eponymous toxin in the late 19th century. As our understanding of the immune system has evolved, its role in the fight against cancer has become increasingly apparent. There have been some monumental milestones that helped shape cancer treatment as it stands today, including Steven Rosenberg's trials of tumor-infiltrating lymphocytes in the 1980s, Hans Kolb's cure of leukemia with donor T cells in the 1990s, and the discovery of checkpoint blockade, which led to Jim Allison's 2018 Nobel Prize and the explosion of the field of immunotherapy.

The focus on immunotherapy puts us at risk for forgetting that the principal role of the immune system is tumor surveillance: the elimination of developing diseases before we are even aware of the danger. Cancer arises from the uncontrolled growth of tumor cells, which have evaded immune surveillance, and immunotherapies are aimed at restoring the body's natural anticancer responses. Nevertheless, despite some groundbreaking results, current immunotherapies remain effective in only a minority of patients.

The reason is that most such therapies target only one of the two sides of the immune system, the adaptive response, and not the innate response. Now many immunotherapists are beginning to understand that broadening our therapeutic options to target the innate response as well will give patients the best chance of beating their disease.

Adaptive immunity, also referred to as acquired immunity, is an antigen-specific immune response that can kill cancer cells and then generate an immunological memory of each tumor-related antigen. This creates a reservoir of immune cells that are able to respond to cancer cells expressing the same specific antigen should it reappear. Adaptive immunity consists of T and B lymphocytes, which lyse tumor cells and generate antibodies to some of the tumor antigens. The process of adaptive immunity is the foundation of vaccinations such as the HPV vaccine, which targets the virus responsible for most cases of cervical cancer.

Why is innate immunotherapy likely to improve outcomes? Innate immunity is our body's first line of defense against infection and cancer. Around 10 percent of the lymphocytes in our peripheral bloodstream are part of the innate response, and 95 percent of those are natural killer (NK) cells. Each of these innate killer cells can recognize, target and kill harmful cells through recognition of proteins and glycoproteins, which are expressed on "stressed" cells, such as tumor and virally infected cells.

In contrast to the adaptive immunity's antigen-specific T cell responses, the innate system is relatively nonspecific and can provide a rapid response. Whereas some of the earliest cellular immunotherapy trials in cancer were directed at innate immunity, many believed that the innate response is inadequate for the control of cancer and instead redirected therapies to focus on the T cell–mediated adaptive immunity.

Clinically, innate and adaptive immunity work together to protect us from infection and cancer, yet our understanding of innate immunity remains relatively poor compared with the adaptive responses. This is partly because adaptive immunity was not discovered until the 1970s and partly because of the technical difficulties in studying NK cell biology compared with T and B cells. The importance of the innate response is accepted in invertebrates, which lack adaptive immunity. It is clearly essential for humans too.

Human NK cells are evolutionarily conserved and even share many molecules with NK cells from invertebrates such as leeches and sea urchins. From the early days of HIV infection, we saw that patients with a fundamentally damaged adaptive immune system were still protected by their innate immune system and succumbed only to some intracellular bacterial infections and rare tumors. They did not die from common infections or uncontrolled tumors.

Today we have a great deal of supporting evidence for the importance of NK cells and the innate response in protection from cancer. Cancer cells are constantly arising in our bodies as a consequence of random genetic mutations, some of which give a cell a survival or proliferation advantage. These random changes are mostly novel and have never been presented to the adaptive immune system. The only cells able to detect the "stress" signals of a tumor cell that is dividing too frequently are NK cells, which can eliminate tumor cells before they become a clinically detectable cancer.

A Japanese study published in 2000 measured the resting NK cell response to a single cancer cell line in more than 3,500 healthy people on a single day of their life and then followed them all for more than 11 years. Those with the weakest resting NK cell function on the single test day had a statistically significantly increased incidence of succumbing to any form of cancer over the period of follow-up. The importance of innate immune surveillance is also seen in NK cell–deficient mice, which generate malignant lymphomas spontaneously.

Far from being the poor, unsophisticated relative of the adaptive immune response, innate immunity is central to survival. As we increase our understanding of the innate immune response and discover how to best manipulate it, NK cell therapies alone will provide even greater advances in immunotherapy for cancer. Alongside treatments involving the adaptive immune response, they will enable us to target cancer better than ever before."

The views expressed are those of the author(s) and are not necessarily those of Scientific American.

About the Author

Mark Lowdell is chief scientific officer of INmune Bio, an immunotherapy company developing treatments to reprogram the innate immune system to fight disease.

What's Next after Creating a Cancer-Prevention Vaccine?

By Dina Fine Maron

Imagine a vaccine that protects against more than a half-dozen types of cancer–and has a decade of data and experience behind it.

We have one. It's the human papillomavirus (HPV) vaccine, and it was approved for the U.S. market back in June 2006. It can prevent almost all cervical cancers and protect against cancers of the mouth, throat, and anus. It also combats the sexually transmitted genital warts that some forms of the virus can cause.

On Wednesday, two researchers who completed fundamental work on these vaccines received one of this year's prestigious Lasker Awards, a group of medical prizes sometimes called the "American Nobels." Douglas Lowy and John Schiller, whose research provided the basis for the HPV vaccine, were selected alongside a researcher who separately unraveled key aspects of metabolic control of cell growth. Planned Parenthood was also given an award, for its public service. Lowy and Schiller, who both work at the U.S. National Cancer Institute (NCI), received the Lasker for their research on animal and human papillomaviruses–work that enabled the development of a vaccine against HPV-16 type, a form of the virus that fuels many HPV malignancies. The duo's experiments proved that the vaccine is effective in animals, and they also conducted the first clinical trial of an HPV-16 vaccine in humans. That gave pharmaceutical companies the evidence they needed to invest in their own vaccines designed to protect against multiple kinds of HPV, and ultimately led to the versions administered around the world today.

Yet HPV shots have had a difficult run. Despite overwhelming evidence of their safety and effectiveness, in some developed countries–including the U.S.–HPV inoculations face opposition from individuals and groups that fear the shots are still too new and unproved to use on their children. The HPV vaccine also faces another hurdle beyond other routine pediatric shots: the virus is transmitted via sexual contact–which some parents and communities believe teens should not or will not have, and thus that the shots should not be mandatory. (The U.S. Centers for Disease Control and Prevention [CDC] currently recommends administering two doses of the vaccines to children 11 to 12 years old, administered at least six months apart.)

Scientific American spoke with Schiller, a virologist, about his and Lowy's award-winning HPV research, their future plans, and how to combat anti-vaccine attitudes.

[*An edited transcript of the interview follows.*]

Q: What's the biggest hurdle to getting more coverage with the HPV vaccine?

A: The biggest problem is actually not in the West or most developed countries; it is in the lower- and middle-income countries because of availability there and vaccine prices that limit availability. In those settings vaccine acceptance is actually very high. But those settings present the biggest problem, since some 85 percent of cervical cancers occur in low-resource settings. In the more developed countries there are many different factors involved [in vaccine hesitancy], and they differ by country. In the U.S. it is more about fear of vaccines in general. And there are some issues with HPV vaccines specifically related to this being about a sexually transmitted disease.

Q: So far, more than 270 million doses of HPV vaccines have been distributed worldwide. But in the United States, by 2015 only 28 percent of teen males and 42 percent of teen girls had received the full course of three shots then recommended by the CDC. How can the science community help combat HPV vaccine hesitancy?

A: There are quite a few studies that show one of the biggest issues is that the vaccine is not being promoted sufficiently by pediatricians and general practitioners. If you look at other vaccines like for meningitis and hepatitis B–which are also administered to adolescents and could be given in the same visit as HPV–they are given at greater rates than HPV. So, there is some disconnect in communication between pediatricians and parents there. Part of the problem here is that the HPV vaccine is a prophylactic vaccine to prevent a disease–cervical cancer–that those providers never see. Obstetrician-gynecologists see it, but pediatricians don't, which is the opposite of most other childhood or pediatric vaccines. Right now it's being singled out as something special instead of treated as a routine childhood or adolescent vaccine. But we've had this vaccine for 10 years now and it's not the new kid on the block anymore.

Q: Mounting evidence suggests that among people who feel vaccines are unsafe, any new data showing that they are really safe does not move the needle to convince them. So, what can be done?

A: My feeling is that there is a certain percentage of people who, no matter what facts you present to them, they are just not going to be convinced. Quite frankly it doesn't pay to spend a lot of resources trying to convince that relatively small fraction. What we need to focus on is a much larger fraction of the population who aren't having their kids vaccinated for reasons like convenience–like it's a hassle–or they just need a bit more information to make them comfortable. People against all vaccines, those people would not be convinced to get an HPV vaccine so it's not worth spending a lot of resources on them. I think one of the things that would increase HPV vaccine coverage would be allowing people to get them at their local CVS. I'm not an expert on this, but I have a daughter who as a teen spent much more time at the local CVS than at her local Kaiser clinic. Different states have different laws about which vaccines can and can't be delivered at pharmacies–but if someone could go get an HPV vaccine at the same place they get their flu vaccine, presumably it would lead to an uptick.

Q: I see you studied molecular biology as an undergrad at the University of Wisconsin–Madison. Did you always want to work on vaccines?

A: No, absolutely not. When I first started out I was an academic purist and thought you should study knowledge for its own sake. I was fascinated by molecular biology. When I first heard about the way metabolism works in bacteria, plants, and humans, that just wowed me because that was a common feature of all life. I just wanted to study that. I thought people who did translational work were sort of selling out to the man–this was in the 1970s. I didn't get interested in vaccines until much later. Now, I'm very fascinated with translational research.

Q: So, what changed?

A: It was a very gradual thing. To this day we still do basic research, and it's still intrinsically valuable to do basic research because you don't know when it will lead to a transformational breakthrough.

Q: What led you to work on HPV?

A: When I had just joined the field, suddenly there was this discovery that made papilloma viruses important for human health as opposed to just an nderstanding of how cells become cancerous. I had joined Doug Lowy's lab at the National Cancer Institute as a postdoc back in 1983, and the second lecture I went to there was by Harald zur Hausen–who later won the Nobel Prize–and his lecture was saying "eureka! We found a virus that seems to cause 50 percent of cervical cancers"–and that virus turned out to be a human papilloma virus strain, HPV-16. So basically we went from looking at a model about how a normal cell transforms to become carcinogenic to something probably involved in causing human cancer. It was somewhat serendipitous.

Q: What are you working on now?

A: One thing we are doing at the NCI, and cosponsored by the Bill & Melinda Gates Foundation, is testing if one dose of HPV vaccine is enough to provide long-term protection. It would be transformative, especially in the developing country setting, if you could just have one dose at a younger age. This new trial is going to be done in Costa Rica in collaboration with the Costa Rican government. That's the site where we had done a prior pilot trial that suggested one dose may be enough.

We are also looking into cancer immunotherapy work. It turns out that these virus-like particles that we work with for the HPV vaccine–these are typically the outer shell of a virus, like from the HPV-16 strain or other animal, or human papilloma virus particles–have a unique ability to infect tumor cells and bind to them specifically. So we are using that knowledge to develop cancer therapies that are broad-spectrum. It turns out these cancers, like melanoma, do bind these particles, specifically.

One other thing we are doing is trying to develop vaccines that would treat herpes simplex infections and HPV infections in the female genital tract. Again, this would take advantage of these virus-like particles' structures.

Q: Last year I interviewed Michael Sofia, who won a Lasker Award for his hepatitis C vaccine work. The name of that vaccine, sofosbuvir–brand name Sovaldi–is a nod to his last name. But the National Institutes of Health (NIH) do a lot of early-stage research, and then it's passed off to private companies that develop it further. Your name isn't part of the HPV vaccines Gardasil or Cervarix, for example. Is it frustrating doing a lot of that behind-the-scenes work?

A: It's funny because I would never have thought of that. It would have never entered my mind to name a vaccine after ourselves. We are so used to doing this translational work. My job is to move a project along so it's interesting enough for a company to invest hundreds of millions of dollars for the benefit of large numbers of people. NIH doesn't have the money to do phase III trials for lots of drugs, and even if they did it wouldn't lead to all the drugs we need–because NIH wouldn't have the money to develop them. This translational and basic research is what NIH does best. That work is way too fraught with failure for companies to do it all. It has to be done in the public sector, and then when things look more promising companies can take it over.

Q: What advice would you offer someone considering becoming a scientist now?

A: It's got to be a passion because being a scientist–especially early in your career–is more a lifestyle than occupation. You have to really want to do it, because there is a lot of uncertainty–especially about running your own lab and getting funding. Success and failure can be on a knife's edge sometimes. The other thing is that you need to be strategic about thinking of what you want to go into, and that's hard for young people because they don't have the perspective: There are some fields just opening up ripe for discoveries. And there are some areas that are very mature, that we have been working on for a long time, where there are a lot of scientists working already–so the chances of making a big impact are lower. From my own life, this is like when we started with human papilloma viruses. When I went into this field, we had just been given the tools to study them and so it seemed like a great opportunity to get involved. In some ways it's best if you can pick an emerging field with new tools to answer big questions. But you have to pick something you are really interested in and go with it.

The other thing I'd say is read a lot. Now with PubMed and access to all these journals there is no excuse for not knowing the background in something that basically has already been done. Young people tend to want to get out and do experiments, but a few days searching PubMed may save someone years of work trying to reinvent the wheel.

Q: Right now, what would you say is the biggest challenge—or one of the biggest challenges—that needs to be solved?

A: That's a really tough one. I think as scientists we are all sort of locked into the things we study. I could say cancer, obviously. But Alzheimer's is something we obviously need to solve. HIV infection. All these different things. One of the things that really needs to be solved in terms of the whole scientific enterprise now is stable funding. Right now we are in a situation where there are too many good scientists—especially young scientists—competing for a limited pot of money. So you lose some good people because there's not enough money to go around. Also, people are forced to do relatively mundane things that are really a methodological extension of something they've done before instead of something truly transformative that would have a large chance of failure. Grant reviewers are looking at something likely to succeed and move the field incrementally, or something transformative that may have a high chance of failure, and have to make those decisions. This is an issue across the sciences. The obvious solution would be to have more funding, but then that raises the question about how to do that. And I'm not a politician.

Q: What, if anything, does this Lasker Award do for your work?

A: Quite honestly, probably nothing, because one of the nice things about being part of intramural research [at NIH] is that I have stable funding. I've had six people in my lab for the last 25 years, so this won't lead to more grants or me doubling the size of my lab, or anything like that. I'm happy with my moderate-sized lab and collaborations with a lot of great people. That's why I'm here. Every four years we have a site visit, which is a retrospective review of "what have you done for us lately," and if it's reasonable I will continue to get funding. So the award won't affect my research career much at all.

Q: Right now, some in the scientific community fear amid this political climate that facts matter less than they once did and thus science matters less. What's your take on that?

A: Obviously, my perspective is science matters a lot. I really can't comment on what's happening in the country overall—and whether this is something that is pervasive where science is really held in less esteem, or it's that there is a vocal minority being heard a lot now. I would hope it's the latter.

About the Author

Dina Fine Maron, formerly an associate editor at Scientific American, *is now a wildlife trade investigative reporter at* National Geographic.

Could Immunotherapy Treat Diseases Besides Cancer?

By Karen Weintraub

Immunotherapy has transformed cancer care. Now the tools and new knowledge created by this strategy for treating disease by stimulating the body's immune system are beginning to be employed for everything from fighting autoimmune illnesses to preventing tissue rejection in organ transplants.

Although still mostly confined to scientific labs, the use of this approach outside of cancer has tremendous potential, researchers say, because the immune system is fundamentally involved in every organ and in many health conditions. "The opportunity exists to move what we call the immunorevolution beyond cancer," says Jonathan Epstein, a cardiologist and chief scientific officer for the University of Pennsylvania Health System (Penn Medicine).

In one type of cancer immunotherapy, immune cells called T cells are removed from the body and engineered to target cells that are only found in cancers. The engineered cells, called chimeric antigen receptor T cells (CAR-Ts), have proved exceedingly effective against some types of blood cancers, particularly acute lymphocytic leukemia. Scientists have now started engineering T cells to attack other disease-related cells.

Cancer was a logical first step for immunotherapies, says Marcela Maus, director of cellular immunotherapy at the Massachusetts General Hospital's Cancer Center and an assistant professor at Harvard Medical School. The need for life-extending therapies in cancer is indisputable. There is a willingness to take risks to fight tumors that might otherwise be fatal, she says. Doctors are likely to be more cautious in fighting autoimmune diseases, which can be terrible but also have some existing–if imperfect–treatments. Now that the immunotherapy work has proved so successful in cancer, it makes sense to push it into other illnesses, Maus says.

A group led by Aimee Payne, a dermatologist at Penn Medicine, is currently preparing for human trials using reengineered T cells to treat an autoimmune-triggered skin disease called pemphigus. In one subform of the affliction that affects about 4,000 Americans, the immune system produces antibodies against proteins that hold the skin together, resulting in painful, debilitating blisters. Payne and her colleagues direct engineered T cells to destroy the immune cells that make these antibodies, and their work has shown promise in animals. Payne says she got the idea for this approach from all the attention successful CAR-Ts were receiving at Penn Medicine. It seemed so simple in retrospect: "You're like, 'Why didn't we think of this earlier?'" she adds. Others had tried to target the antibodies that cause this skin disease before, without success. Payne says she is more optimistic about the engineered T cells she is using, which she calls CAAR-T cells (with an extra "A"), for chimeric autoantibody receptor T cells, because they can make more copies of themselves, so their effects could be long-lasting.

Even decades-old immunotherapies are inspiring present-day work. In Paris, David Klatzmann, an immunologist at Sorbonne University, is experimenting with treating autoimmune disorders with low levels of interleukin-2 (IL-2), an immune-signaling molecule first used to treat cancer in the mid-1980s. Back then, high doses of IL-2 proved effective in a small fraction of metastatic tumors—mainly kidney cancer and melanoma—but caused terrible side effects. Klatzmann's research suggests low doses may be able to treat a wide range of autoimmune conditions by boosting levels of a type of cell called a regulatory T cell, or Treg, which naturally muzzles the immune response. He uses immunotherapy to suppress the immune system—the opposite of what cancer researchers do.

Klatzmann's university and two other French institutions hold a patent on low-dose IL-2, and he is hosting a meeting in November with other researchers and pharmaceutical companies who are exploring its potential for a wide range of diseases. He says IL-2 is the only molecule that preferentially activates Tregs, and "there is Treg insufficiency in almost every autoimmune disease and also inflammatory disease," including atherosclerosis, or the hardening of the arteries. He is now testing his approach in phase II clinical trials for autoimmune illnesses, including lupus, type 1 diabetes and multiple sclerosis.

Jerome Ritz, who runs a cell-manufacturing lab at the Dana-Farber Cancer Institute, says CAR-Ts made with engineered Tregs could also be used against inflammation or in transplant patients to prevent rejection. Stem cell transplants can cure some blood cancers but can also lead to life-threatening graft versus host disease, in which immune cells from the donor attack the recipient. It should be possible to engineer so-called CAR-Tregs to induce tolerance to recipient cells–or even to an entire transplanted organ to prevent rejection, says Ritz, who is also a professor at Harvard Medical School.

Penn Medicine's Epstein recently engineered T cells in mice to attack cells that produce scar tissue after the heart suffers damage. Known as fibrosis, this scarring initially keeps the heart from rupturing, but it can also impair the organ's ability to fill with blood and pump efficiently. Epstein's approach worked in mice, reducing the amount of scar tissue, a study recently published in *Nature* shows. He hopes to test the method in larger animals.

But some experts remain skeptical. Eric Topol, a cardiologist and executive vice president of the Scripps Research Institute, says he doubts Epstein's approach will work in humans. "It's interesting science, but it's a long way off from having implications for people with heart disease," Topol says. Many treatments that work in mice do not translate well in people, he notes. And although fibrosis is clearly a problem in heart failure, it is not as clear that targeting fibrotic tissue will help patients. He also worries about the safety of any intervention that might affect the beating of the heart. "If you muck around with it, you could actually engender serious heart-rhythm problems," he says, "which can be deadly."

Even if this specific work never pans out, Epstein and others say the larger approach is still valid: learning how to manipulate the immune system to fight cancer has taught researchers information they can now use to fight diseases ranging from infections to arthritis.

Maus agrees: "I think we are definitely in a moment where this kind of science, this kind of potential product–engineered T cells–is transformational. They can be applied in so many different settings and diseases," she says. But "I think it's still a little bit early to know whether it's going to be a commercial product for patients."

About the Author

Karen Weintraub is a staff writer at USA Today, *where she covers COVID-19, vaccine development, and other health issues.*

Fighting the Opioid Crisis with Vaccines and Better Chemistry

By Dina Fine Maron

Drug-overdose deaths now exceed the number of people dying in car crashes in the U.S. They dwarf deaths from gunshots. And for opioids–which led to some 33,000 deaths in 2015–the numbers are continuing to rise. Preliminary data for 2016 suggests there were more than 50,000 opioid overdose deaths.

The surge is renewing public focus on efforts to develop vaccines that would block the drugs' euphoric effects and therapies that would tamp down the extreme withdrawal symptoms that can leave an addict feeling like they will die unless they get a fix. "One of the exciting things that [scientists are] actually working on is a vaccine for addiction," said Tom Price, Health and Human Services secretary, in a press conference last week. Opioid vaccine work is "incredibly exciting," he added. But not everyone is so sanguine.

To better understand if the White House's enthusiasm is warranted, *Scientific American* interviewed the lead investigators of the top three opioid vaccine candidates–and came away with some sobering news: None of those candidate vaccines have made it to human trials, which suggests it may be many years before they reach patients–if at all. Nevertheless, some potential approaches are showing initial promise.

Like other vaccines, an opioid inoculation would cue the body to generate antibodies–proteins normally associated with fighting diseases–only here they would be specifically directed against opioid molecules. Each vaccine would focus on only one type of opioid. Take heroin, for example: If someone received a heroin vaccine and then used the drug, instead of experiencing a high, the drug and its psychoactive metabolites would be quickly bound up by antibodies that would prevent them from reaching the brain. That would stop them from getting to receptors that might normally make the heroin user both feel good and also simultaneously depress breathing–the leading cause of overdose deaths. In short, an effective opioid vaccine could potentially save lives. Yet every opioid vaccine effort–dating back to the 1970s–has failed.

The most advanced opioid vaccine candidate is a heroin vaccine designed by scientists at the Scripps Research Institute. That team, headed by chemistry and immunology professor Kim Janda, recently published promising research showing the vaccine could neutralize varying doses of heroin in rhesus monkeys without any problematic side effects–making it the first opioid vaccine to get to that point. Four monkeys were given three doses of vaccine each. During the first month following vaccination the treatment helped block heroin's effects, and it continued to provide some degree of protection for more than eight months. Notably, the vaccine only worked against heroin–not other opioids. Moreover, two of the monkeys that had also received the vaccine during an initial pilot study seven months earlier were better able to neutralize heroin's effects after the second round of shots, which is good news–suggesting inoculations might be more effective with future booster shots. "We think we have a pretty good [drug] cocktail right now. Our confidence is bolstered by our nonhuman primate studies," Janda says. But he notes that other vaccines, including one for cocaine, previously looked promising in animals but did not elicit high enough levels of antibodies to provide protection in humans.

Several other teams are developing candidate vaccines. Two separate drugs designed to combat prescription painkiller oxycodone and heroin have been in the works for years at the Minneapolis Medical Research Foundation (MMRF), but those vaccines are still only being tested in rodents. "For our group and others it will take years before we reach the market," says Marco Pravetoni, who is co-leading the work at MMRF. Now his team is focused on manufacturing pharmaceutical-grade vaccines that would be eligible for U.S. Food and Drug Administration testing, and they are looking for possible industry partners to speed up the process to product development, he says.

Meanwhile, the U.S. Army also has another candidate heroin vaccine that it hopes to eventually couple with an experimental HIV vaccine it is working on–to simultaneously reduce disease and fight addiction. That vaccine, which is also in rodent testing, has been licensed to Opiant Pharmaceuticals –formerly Lightlake Therapeutics–the company that helped net FDA approval for the overdose antidote intranasal naloxone (Narcan), says Gary Matyas, chief of the Adjuvants and Formulations Section at Walter Reed Army Institute of Research and head of its opioid vaccine research.

Despite the seemingly slow progress, there have been significant improvements in opioid vaccine development in recent decades, says Ivan Montoya, acting director of the Division of Therapeutics and Medical Consequences at the National Institute on Drug Abuse (NIDA). "Newer vaccines are able to stimulate the immune system more efficiently," he says. "So the production of antibodies is better than what it was in the past." And historically, the holdup has not just been the technology of vaccine development, he notes. There were relatively effective medication-assisted interventions like methadone that also put opioid vaccine research on the back burner until relatively recently. "But right now the opioid crisis issue is going beyond the interventions we have," he says, noting those medications are not always available or completely effective.

An option with more immediate promise than vaccine candidates may be introducing more options to treat withdrawal symptoms, Montoya says. The FDA is currently reviewing one treatment, lofexidine, which is already approved in the U.K. and will hopefully be approved in the U.S. "soon," he says. The drug, which was partly supported by the NIDA, is being developed specifically for the treatment of opioid withdrawal syndrome–a troubling constellation of symptoms that can include body aches, racing heart, nausea, and vomiting. Whereas medications like methadone or buprenorphine–which essentially trick the brain into thinking it is still getting the abused drug–can relieve the withdrawal symptoms and psychological cravings, if lofexidine is given a regulatory green light, "this will be the first and only medication approved by the FDA for the specific indication of treatment of opioid withdrawal," Montoya says. (The FDA declined to comment on whether the drug was under review or its potential timing.) Right now there is also a third medication-assisted treatment called naltrexone, which can help neutralize heroin's high but would likely not be as long-acting or cost-effective as a vaccine.

Opioid experts say they see other obvious benefits for vaccine development. "One of the advantages to a vaccine would potentially be compliance related–if the vaccine lasts several months, that person wouldn't need to take a medication or treatment during that time," says Stanford University anesthesiology professor David Clark, a member of the National Academies of Sciences, Engineering, and Medicine committee that reviewed available opioid interventions and put out a report on how to combat the opioid crisis last month. Another benefit of inoculations, he says, might be that substance abusers may prefer them to methadone or buprenorphine–medical opioids that some people are reluctant to use because they believe they are trading one opioid addiction for another. (Unlike heroin, however, the medications are administered in a controlled setting at specific doses. They have gradual onset and produce stable levels of the drug in the brain–which NIDA says helps the cycle of drug crashes and cravings and helps reduce the desire to use opioids.)

But because the three experimental vaccine candidates from Scripps, the MMRF, and the Army have not been used in humans, it is impossible to know how safe they would be and how they would operate in the real world. One major concern is if a person takes a heroin vaccine, he may turn to a different opioid for a high. That's why, right now, there is a need to expand the use of available, proved techniques including medication-assisted treatments and counseling to help fight the opioid crisis, Clark says.

"Whether those vaccines will be truly effective–maintaining a high enough titer of antibodies against the illicit opioid to protect them from the drug–that's quite a challenge. They may also be expensive and it seems they would require frequent revaccination and boosters," Clark says. "I wouldn't want to lose perspective on deploying what we have–which could be used more effectively–while just waiting on the promise of a vaccine."

About the Author

Dina Fine Maron, formerly an associate editor at Scientific American, *is now a wildlife trade investigative reporter at* National Geographic.

The Next Wave of Immuno-Oncology

By Rafael Amado, Elliot Norry

In 2017 the first immuno-oncology cell therapies, known as chimeric antigen receptor T cells, or CAR T, were approved by the U.S. Food and Drug Administration. Immuno-oncology cell therapy is a field that leverages the immune system by modifying, and thereby enhancing, immune cells to target cancer. It accomplishes this by interdicting pathways that maintain checks and balances on cellular elements of the immune system, thereby disrupting the tolerance of the body to the growth and spread of cancer.

CAR T therapies have had unprecedented success in blood cancers, such as certain leukemias and lymphomas. They have shown high response rates and redefined the treatment of patients who have exhausted other options. Their therapeutic success relies on an antibody fragment that binds to a surface protein on leukemias and lymphomas; one such protein is known as CD19. The antibody fragment is linked to stimulatory and signaling molecules that fire on binding of the antibody with the CD19 molecule, thereby activating the T cells and making them destroy the cancer cell.

Solid Tumor Challenges

CAR T therapies have shown limited success in solid tumors because they do not typically express a molecule on their surface that is unique to the tumor and not common to normal tissue. Coupled with the complex matrix in which cancer cells grow, this makes it challenging to develop cellular therapies for solid tumors.

One way to overcome this challenge is to target proteins expressed inside the cell rather than large cell-surface proteins. This kind of immune response involves the activation of T cells against a part of an internal protein that the T cells see as foreign. These protein fragments, known as peptides, dock with protein structures on the cell surface known as major histocompatibility antigens (MHCs), which are the cellular network that governs the presentation of self versus nonself peptides and lets T cells distinguish friend from foe.

T cells are some of the "surveyors and assassins" of the immune system. They have T cell receptors (TCRs) on their surface, and they circulate through the body, binding foreign peptides on the surface of cells that are infected by foreign organisms such as viruses and bacteria. When a cell is infected, bits of that organism's protein make it to the surface, docking with the right MHC. Surveying T cells can see these proteins through their TCRs and kill them to prevent propagation of the infection.

Yet cancer cells have proteins that look similar to the body's own, not like foreign proteins, which fosters an ability to evade the immune system. This makes it difficult to effectively target tumors with our body's own naturally occurring TCRs. When cancer cells develop mutations, they may present novel, aberrant peptides, but often the malignant cell and other elements of the tumor dampen the T cell response by interfering with the molecular network that regulates how T cells function. The unraveling of some of the proteins that regulate T cell function against tumor cells resulted in two scientists sharing the 2018 Nobel Prize in Physiology or Medicine.

The Potential of Enhanced Receptors

Companies are now exploring how to enhance the body's naturally occurring TCRs to target solid tumors. Engineering TCRs to have optimal affinity for the docking peptide enables the receptors to more easily identify proteins from cancer cells that would otherwise not be recognized as foreign.

These engineered TCRs can be put into a patient's own T cells, which are then returned to the patient. These newly enhanced T cells can kill tumors, multiply and attack more cancer cells than a patient's naturally occurring T cells.

Biopharmaceutical company Adaptimmune uses its unique SPEAR (specific peptide enhanced affinity receptor) T cell platform to engineer TCRs that can recognize cancer proteins on solid tumors.

Future Immuno-Oncology

There is still more to come from the immuno-oncology cell therapy field with respect to utilizing TCRs, given that many solid tumors recur and become incurable. This is why Adaptimmune is conducting clinical trials with multiple engineered TCRs across a broad range of solid tumors. The company is also investigating next-generation TCRs armed with molecules to further improve the engineered T cells' ability to target and destroy solid tumors. These enhanced approaches will likely lead to longer-lasting antitumor responses.

Patients in dire need of novel treatment options are the driving force pushing Adaptimmune and many companies in the life sciences industry to continue the quest to eradicate metastatic cancer. The field has come a long way, and its potential appears boundless as scientists unravel the intricate interplay between cancer and anticancer immunity.

Update: Since this article was published three years ago, Adaptimmune has made great progress with its engineered SPEAR T cells for solid tumors. Later in 2022 we plan to file a biologics license application request to the FDA for approval of our lead product, afamitresgene autoleucel (afami-cel), for the treatment of synovial sarcoma. Afami-cel uses an engineered TCR to target the cancer/testis antigen MAGE-A4. A phase 2 trial of the therapy has shown a response rate of 36 percent in synovial sarcoma. This rare and difficult-to-treat cancer presents a high unmet medical need, for which afami-cel is a potential game changer.

We have also launched several trials of next-generation SPEAR T cells targeting MAGE-A4. An early trial has shown promising initial responses in synovial sarcoma and in esophagogastric junction, ovarian, head and neck, and bladder cancers. Based on these responses, we initiated a late-phase trial for gastroesophageal cancers, and we plan to launch one for ovarian cancer later this year.

About the Authors

Rafael Amado is a former president of research and development at Adaptimmune. He is currently chief medical officer of Allogene Therapeutics.

Elliot Norry has served as Adaptimmune's chief medical officer since January 2020. Prior to that, he was the company's acting chief marketing officer, vice president, and head of clinical safety and pharmacovigilance, as well as the leader of its ADP-A2AFP program.

Vanquishing Diabetes

By Kristen M. Drescher, Steven Tracy

About three decades ago, a British epidemiologist named David P. Strachan proposed a simple, if counterintuitive, idea to explain why hay fever, eczema, and asthma had become increasingly common over the preceding century. Strachan linked rising rates of these allergic illnesses in the U.K. with improvements in living standards since the industrial revolution—in particular, a sharp drop in the number of infections experienced in early childhood. He surmised that exposure to bacteria and viruses in the first years of life (provided an infant survived them) somehow protected against these conditions showing up later.

Although Strachan's original hunch, now commonly known as the hygiene hypothesis, concerned allergic disorders, researchers have since used its basic tenet—exposure, or lack thereof, to environmental influences—to explain historical increases in various other conditions as well. These include poliomyelitis, multiple sclerosis, and type 1 diabetes. Numerous epidemiological surveys have revealed certain escalating disease patterns as industrialization spread from Europe to North America and beyond. Wherever the rate of childhood infections (and mortality) fell, the incidence of several previously rare illnesses started to rise—albeit not uniformly and not all at once.

Major polio outbreaks first began to appear in the late 1800s. The incidence of multiple sclerosis, in which the immune system attacks the protective covering around particular nerve cells, doubled in certain parts of the world in the second half of the 20th century. Type 1 diabetes, which occurs when the body mistakenly destroys cells in the pancreas that make the hormone insulin (which enables the body to use glucose for energy), started creeping up in the first half of the 1900s and rose dramatically in the 1950s.

Exactly how early exposure to various viruses or bacteria can protect against the emergence of a number of seemingly unrelated illnesses remains unclear. Somehow the infections enable the developing body to learn how to deal with pathogens. Further, the absence of exposure to these microbes can prompt the body to attack itself. In particular, a substantial collection of research implicates a fairly large group of pathogens called enteroviruses in the surge of polio and type 1 diabetes.

Unlike the far more common type 2 diabetes–often tied to weight gain in adulthood–type 1 diabetes usually strikes before the age of 20. Our experiments on mice that are prone to spontaneously acquiring type 1 diabetes have revealed a complex mechanism whereby the same strains of enteroviruses can either prevent or instigate the illness, depending on the age of the mouse when it is infected. Assuming our results are confirmed in humans, a vaccine based on a group of viruses commonly excreted in feces could potentially prevent type 1 diabetes in many individuals.

A Century of Clues

Our research began with a fundamental question, similar to the one Strachan had addressed: Why was type 1 diabetes so rare in the past and yet a scourge by the 1950s? In ancient times, Greek, Arab, Indian, and Chinese physicians all described a rare cluster of symptoms–including rapid weight loss, abnormal thirst, and urine that tasted sweet when sampled–that were almost certainly an outcome of type 1 diabetes. Extrapolating from individual hospital data, researchers calculate that about one or two in every 100,000 children under the age of 15 developed type 1 diabetes in the early 1900s. Today that number is closer to 20 per 100,000 children in parts of the U.S. and more than 60 per 100,000 in Finland. Disturbingly, these numbers continue to rise.

The increase has not been steady, however. After years of just creeping up in some countries, type 1 diabetes began to soar in the middle of the 20th century. Since then, epidemiologists have calculated an average annual increase of between 3 and 5 percent across the globe. Between 1998 and 2010 the incidence of type 1 diabetes jumped by a shocking 40 percent.

Such a steep rise in such a short time told us that we were not looking at a fundamental change in the human gene pool: DNA does not mutate that rapidly. A variety of different combinations of many genes profoundly increase the risk of an individual acquiring type 1 diabetes. As far as investigators can tell, however, the prevalence of these high-risk genetic profiles has not changed. Instead more and more people with a relatively low genetic predisposition to type 1 diabetes are now suffering from the ailment. Few cases can be linked solely to a genetic disorder. These and other findings, from scientists around the world, strongly suggest that newly emergent environmental factors must be at work.

Various possibilities have been considered over the years–and dismissed. Unlike type 2 diabetes, type 1 cannot be brought on by a person's diet or other health-related habits. More intriguingly, several studies have determined that type 1 diabetes occurs more frequently the farther away one gets from the equator. Might a lack of vitamin D, which is easily produced by the body whenever it is in sunlight, account for such regional variation? That idea soon fell apart, however. Epidemiologists discovered, for instance, that some countries in the far north, such as Finland, had higher rates of type 1 diabetes in regions with more sunlight than in regions with less.

The bulk of the evidence points instead to a viral trigger–probably one or more viruses that occur in sewage or in contaminated drinking water. Numerous studies indicate that enteroviruses–so named because they are normally found in the intestine (*énteron* in ancient Greek)–are the culprits. (Indeed, no substantive data link any other kind of viral or environmental influences to the disease.) Some enteroviruses are able to replicate in the pancreas, inflaming areas adjacent to where the islet cells, which produce insulin, reside. The inflamed regions produce autoimmune T cells. In normal circumstances, our T cells protect the body against invaders. Autoimmune T cells, however, attack the body's own islet cells, destroying their ability to produce insulin and thereby bringing on diabetes.

Researchers have counted more than 100 types of enteroviruses. No single type of enterovirus, however, seems solely responsible for detonating diabetes around the world. Rather scientists have identified a number of candidates, chief among them six enteroviruses called the Coxsackie B viruses, implicated in the precipitation of the ailment. And they do not understand exactly how such infections might provoke the body to attack itself. The process must be complex: epidemiological studies indicate that specific enteroviruses that appear to advance the disorder in some people apparently protect others from developing it in the first place.

Dirty Water

As we evaluated the kinds of experiments that could potentially identify diabetes-causing enteroviruses, we sought clues in a different illness: polio. An often paralyzing childhood affliction, polio is caused by another class of enteroviruses, called polioviruses. These viruses seem to have been around for millennia: an ancient Egyptian stele (a relief carved in a stone slab), now in a Copenhagen museum, appears to depict a polio patient. The terrible condition they engender used to be quite rare, however, until the late 19th century, when sporadic and then annual epidemics suddenly began to occur. Polio killed tens of thousands of children and crippled millions more in the 20th century. As recently as 1988, polio crippled about 1,000 children a day. Thanks to a massive vaccination campaign, polio is now endemic in only two countries.

The hygiene hypothesis helps to explain this sudden surge in polio cases. It is easy to forget that many conveniences of contemporary life in the developed world are only about a century old. Before the widespread installation of municipal water supplies in Europe and North America, people drew water from wells, ponds, or public fountains for all purposes, including drinking, bathing, and washing clothes. Unsurprisingly, drinking water was often contaminated with human or animal waste. The paucity of running water and soap also meant that people could not be as strict about keeping their hands clean after going to the bathroom as they can be today. Consequently, the simple act of preparing a meal or shaking hands could spread germs far and wide.

Thus, nearly everyone, from early life onward, was exposed to polioviruses that had been passed into the environment from human feces. Newborns did not tend to develop the illness, however, because their mothers had developed immunity against the viruses and passed on protective antibodies to both the developing fetuses during pregnancy and the babies during nursing. As infants grew older and stopped nursing, and as maternal antibodies waned, young children began to make their own protective antibodies against the virus because of repeated exposures to it. So although polioviruses were almost ubiquitous, polio itself was uncommon because youngsters were first protected by the mothers' antibodies and were subsequently protected by their own immune system.

This chain of protection, a part of human life for eons, began to break as human populations entered a "cleaner" world. A boy who might have been spared exposure to polioviruses could encounter them later in life, when he had no protective immunity. Such a chance encounter with poliovirus could then lead to paralytic polio—once in every 100 to 200 poliovirus infections. That is probably why President Franklin D. Roosevelt, for example, developed paralytic polio at the age of 39 while on vacation on an island in New Brunswick, Canada.

Doctors in the U.S. alone diagnose 64,000 new cases of type 1 diabetes every year.

Despite polio's grim legacy, we took some consolation from the fact that a vaccine for the viral infection that causes it had proved safe and immensely effective. If researchers can make a vaccine against one type of enterovirus, they should be able to make vaccines against others as well. And if experiments prove that enteroviruses cause type 1 diabetes, the discovery might point to a potential new treatment: namely, a vaccine against type 1 diabetes that would protect those at greatest risk from acquiring the viral infection in the first place.

(We can rule out poliovirus as a cause of type 1 diabetes. Although polio epidemics became commonplace in the 20th century, no parallel outbreaks of type 1 diabetes were observed. In addition, polio has been eradicated from countries where the incidence of type 1 diabetes continues to rise.)

To show that a virus causes a particular disease, one should begin by isolating the virus from the affected tissue. For type 1 diabetes, that is the pancreas. But safely sampling tissues from a human pancreas remains a surgical challenge–which is why such biopsies are seldom performed on people who are otherwise healthy. Furthermore, pinning down the exact moment when the body's immune system starts attacking the pancreas and destroying the insulin-producing islet cells is extremely difficult. By the time it becomes clear that someone has type 1 diabetes, any signs of what may have been an active infection have usually disappeared.

Nevertheless, about 40 published reports convincingly link the presence of various enteroviruses to the onset of type 1 diabetes: either the virus or its genetic material was isolated from patients' postmortem pancreatic tissues. And other studies have shown that some kind of enterovirus infection most likely plays a long-term role in the development of type 1 diabetes.

As it happens, a particular mouse strain, known as the nonobese diabetic (NOD) mouse, acquires type 1 diabetes on its own, without any intervention from investigators. (Curiously, NOD mice maintained in hygienic conditions acquire the disease much faster than those in dirty cages.) We hypothesized that NOD mice resemble humans with a genetic predisposition to type 1 diabetes. Furthermore, unlike most enteroviruses, the Coxsackie B viruses replicate well in mice and had already been linked to type 1 diabetes. All these factors made NOD mice the ideal model for exploring the relation between enteroviruses and type 1 diabetes.

In 2002 we deliberately infected very young NOD mice, otherwise held in sterile environments, with Coxsackie B viruses. We found that the animals were much less likely to develop type 1 diabetes as they aged, compared with uninfected control subjects. These results supported the hypothesis that early exposure to microbes offers a protective effect against developing type 1 diabetes. Intriguingly, that effect was not limited to specific types of Coxsackie B viruses, although some seemed to provide stronger protection than others. Experiments by virologist Heikki Hyöty of Tampere University in Finland and his colleagues have yielded similar outcomes.

We can think of three possible mechanisms by which exposure to enteroviruses when young might prevent the damaging impact of such infections later in life. First, an infection could trigger the development of protective antibodies against that specific type of enterovirus, so subsequent exposure to the same type would not result in disease. (This process mirrors the principle behind the poliovirus vaccines and many other viral vaccines we use today.) Second, because the Coxsackie B viruses are very similar, on a molecular level, to other enteroviruses, they may prompt the body to more rapidly mobilize adequate defenses, even to enteroviruses it has never encountered before. Third, an enterovirus infection may stimulate the production of regulatory immune cells called Tregs. These generally beneficial cells serve as a conscientious police force, suppressing autoimmune T cells that would otherwise harm the host.

To tease apart these diverse mechanisms, we decided to infect the mice at different ages and observe them for at least 30 weeks after the inoculation. After many years of experimentation, we discovered that infecting older NOD mice with Coxsackie B viruses increased, rather than decreased, their likelihood of developing type 1 diabetes. This finding contrasted sharply with what we had observed in young NOD mice.

We concluded that the pancreas had to be already inflamed–meaning that the insulin-producing islet cells had to be under attack by the mouse's own autoimmune T cells to begin with–for an enterovirus to enter the islets and multiply, accelerating the onset of diabetes. In other words, a genetically induced autoimmune attack on the pancreas had to be underway before a Coxsackie B virus infection could hasten the onset of type 1 diabetes. The older the mouse and the worse the inflammation, the faster the illness would take hold—often resulting in full-blown diabetes in a day or two. (In contrast, older mice held in sterile environments developed diabetes weeks later.)

Studies by immunologist Matthias von Herrath of the La Jolla Institute for Immunology in California and his colleagues indicated that enterovirus infections early in life (before an autoimmune attack is launched) can stimulate the production of regulatory T cells, which persist into adulthood. The Tregs suppress the production of autoimmune T cells and thereby protect against type 1 diabetes. But if the pancreas is already inflamed with autoimmune T cells—as would naturally happen in older NOD mice—the virus is able to replicate, damaging the insulin-producing islet cells and precipitating diabetes. In other words, enteroviruses can either protect against or trigger type 1 diabetes in NOD mice, depending on the age at which the infection occurs.

Diabetes Vaccines

Assuming these observations in NOD mice reflect what occurs in humans with a genetic predisposition to type 1 diabetes, how might we exploit them to help such vulnerable individuals? Nobody wishes to return to the days of poor or no hygienic practices. But we should not have to. Based on our experience with poliovirus vaccines, we know that developing safe and effective enterovirus vaccines is feasible.

Generally, antiviral vaccines come in three versions: live but attenuated, killed and subunit. Live, attenuated vaccines were originally generated by passing the virus through cells or an animal host to weaken its ability to cause disease. Such vaccines are regarded as the most proficient at inducing immunity because the viruses replicate in the host and induce a normal immune response. But they can mutate rapidly into a pathogenic strain. Genetic engineering now enables specific areas of a virus's genome to be altered or deleted to limit the likelihood of such reversion, but the risk remains. Killed vaccines inactivate viruses so that they cannot multiply, but they still induce a certain level of immunity in the host. Because the virus does not persist in the body, however, periodic revaccination is usually required. A subunit vaccine uses one or more parts of a virus that are known to stimulate an immune response to produce the desired type of immunity in the person vaccinated. In 2021 mRNA-based vaccines against SARS-CoV-2 were deployed to fight the COVID pandemic and showed excellent results, inducing protective immunity in those vaccinated. Given such success, this technology will, in the near future, be readily adapted to other vaccine targets such as human enteroviruses to prevent infections, as well as to potentially prevent type 1 diabetes.

The bulk of the evidence indicates that no single enterovirus or even a few enteroviruses are involved in the onset of type 1 diabetes throughout the world. Furthermore, the historical evidence indicates that type 1 diabetes was rare when exposure to numerous enteroviruses was a fact of life. We hypothesize, therefore, that vaccination with multiple types of enteroviruses should offer the most protection. Such an approach would simulate the way humans used to accumulate protective immunity to enteroviruses throughout history. The initial vaccine could be a killed-virus one for safely inducing immunity. Thereafter, either inactivated or highly attenuated vaccines could be used as booster doses.

We find it encouraging that a vaccine approach against type 1 diabetes is finally underway. Hyöty's group is working with Finnish biopharma Vactech Oy, for which Hyöty is chair of the board, to develop a vaccine against a single type of Coxsackie B virus and has tested its ability to prevent type 1 diabetes in mice. Phase 1 clinical trials of this killed-virus vaccine in humans began in 2021. Testing it in children–to ensure safety, generation of a protective immune response to the enterovirus and protection from type 1 diabetes–will take upward of a decade. Given that numerous observations suggest that no single strain of enterovirus is involved with type 1 diabetes, we can only remain hopeful that this vaccine will significantly lower the incidence of the disease.

In addition, a remarkable variety of efforts are in the works to reverse type 1 diabetes after its onset. Investigator Paolo Fiorina of Boston Children's Hospital and his colleagues have demonstrated that appropriately manipulated stem cells, when infused into mice, can sometimes reverse type 1 diabetes. Another group, led by Denise Faustman of the Massachusetts General Hospital Immunobiology Laboratory, is investigating the efficacy of the bacillus Calmette-Guérin (BCG) vaccine, normally used to prevent tuberculosis, in undoing the effects of type 1 diabetes. Several research groups in the U.S. and the U.K. have focused on immunization with proinsulin (a precursor of insulin) or the DNA that encodes for it. In particular, a 2017 report from a multi-investigator effort by Mark Peakman of King's College London and his colleagues indicates that a protein fragment from proinsulin can induce beneficial responses in people newly diagnosed with type 1 diabetes.

Doctors in the U.S. alone diagnose 64,000 new cases of type 1 diabetes every year. We need to remember that a vaccine cannot entirely eradicate the disease: some cases seem to occur solely because of the patient's genetic makeup. Refining treatments to improve the quality of life for individuals who can no longer make their own insulin remains important. Even if only a small fraction of participants in vaccine trials are protected from the disease, however, a significant number of people will have better lives. Given how fast the incidence of type 1 diabetes is increasing, the ability to make it as rare as it once was could benefit millions.

About the Authors

Kristen M. Drescher is a professor of medical microbiology and immunology at Creighton University. She studies the role of viruses in autoimmune disease and explores novel therapeutics in treating inflammatory ailments.

Steven Tracy is professor emeritus of pathology and microbiology at the University of Nebraska Medical Center. His research focused on the molecular biology of enteroviruses, as well as on the impact of such pathogens on myocarditis and type 1 diabetes.

Immune Cells Suggest New Alzheimer's Treatment Possibilities

By Jason Ulrich, David M. Holtzman

In 1907 German psychiatrist Alois Alzheimer published a case report of an unusual illness affecting the cerebral cortex. A 51-year-old woman living in an asylum in Frankfurt am Main exhibited symptoms that are all too familiar to the millions of families affected by what is now known as Alzheimer's disease. There was memory loss, confusion, and disorientation.

After the patient died, Alzheimer examined her brain and made a few key observations. First, it was smaller than average, or atrophic, with a corresponding loss of neurons. Next, there were tangles of protein fibers within neurons and deposits of a different protein outside brain cells. For the next 100 years, these two pathological proteins–known as tau and amyloid–were the focus of research into the causes of the disease.

But there was an additional, often forgotten clue that Alzheimer noted in the autopsy. Under the microscope lens, he saw clear changes in the structural makeup of certain nonneuronal cells. Called glia, they constitute roughly half of the brain's cells.

After being studied by only a small number of scientists since Alzheimer's discovery, glia have now entered the spotlight. One type, called microglia, is the main kind of immune cell in the brain and may influence the progression of the disease in different ways during both early and later stages. Microglia might also explain the complex relation between amyloid and tau, the aberrant proteins that lead to neuron degeneration and memory loss.

Research in the past decade has identified new molecular risk factors that implicate these brain immune cells in Alzheimer's disease. Guided by powerful genetic-sequencing methods, we are beginning to gain an understanding of microglia and of the role of the immune system and its inflammatory processes in Alzheimer's.

Although we have learned a lot about the biochemistry of tau and amyloid proteins, as well as about some of the genetic and lifestyle factors that can influence a person's risk of Alzheimer's, there are virtually no treatments to stop or slow the progression of the disease. On June 7 the U.S. Food and Drug Administration approved a new drug, aducanumab, that removes amyloid from the brain. But it is unclear how effective it is in improving patients' waning cognitive skills. More interventions are still needed. Recent insights about microglia have suggested potential new therapies for the disease, and several are being developed now, with some already being tested in clinical trials.

Plaques, Tangles, and Genes

Alzheimer's disease is the leading cause of dementia worldwide, and its multiple pathologies accumulate and converge over the course of decades. Alzheimer's has two distinctive molecular hallmarks. The first is plaques made up of one form of amyloid called beta-amyloid. These peptides, or small proteins, are found in the spaces between cells.

The second is the contorted, or misfolded, forms of the tau protein, to which large numbers of phosphate groups get attached in a process known as hyperphosphorylation. This increase in tau phosphorylation has been linked to increased aggregation and toxicity of the protein. Tau is present in twisted clumps, called neurofibrillary tangles, in the cell bodies of neurons. Some tau also turns up adjacent to amyloid plaques in swollen, damaged axons, the long protrusions from the main bodies of neurons. This form is known as neuritic plaque tau.

Both tau and the larger protein from which amyloid is derived have normal roles in cell functioning that get corrupted by the disease process in people with Alzheimer's. Extensive efforts to understand the pathological forms of amyloid and tau have led to the conclusion that we should consider Alzheimer's in two stages. The first is a presymptomatic phase of 15 to 25 years during which amyloid builds up in the cerebral cortex, the brain's outermost layer, in the absence of cognitive symptoms. In the second phase, tau tangles develop in the cortex, and neurodegeneration begins, with cognitive dysfunction appearing as brain cells die.

The Alzheimer's research community has known for decades that genetic risk factors strongly influence a person's likelihood of developing Alzheimer's and that genes provide valuable insight into mechanisms underlying the disease. The foremost risk gene associated with Alzheimer's is APOE. It encodes the protein apolipoprotein E, which is involved in fat and cholesterol metabolism. (The alphanumeric designations for genes are typically italicized, whereas those for the proteins they encode are presented as regular text.)

The gene's association with Alzheimer's, first reported in 1993, relates to one version of it, known as an allele, that dramatically increases the risk of illness. The three common APOE alleles in the human population are APOE2, APOE3 and APOE4. APOE3 is the most common, constituting approximately 78 percent of all alleles, followed by APOE4 at around 14 percent and APOE2 at around 8 percent. Every person has two APOE alleles, and about 25 percent of people carry at least one APOE4 allele. But among those with Alzheimer's, about 60 percent have at least one APOE4 allele.

People with a single allele of APOE4 have a threefold to fourfold increased risk of developing Alzheimer's, and individuals with two copies of APOE4 have an approximately 12-fold increased risk compared with people who have two alleles of APOE3. APOE4 carriers have earlier and more abundant deposition of amyloid plaques because their version of apolipoprotein E decreases clearance of beta-amyloid from the brain and facilitates aggregation of the protein. Conversely, people who are APOE2 carriers are at lower risk for developing Alzheimer's and are much less likely to develop amyloid pathology.

Despite the strength of APOE4's effect, it does not account for all of the genetic susceptibility to Alzheimer's. Geneticists have doggedly pursued other risk factors that might explain this "missing heritability," using advances in gene-sequencing technology to screen thousands of people for changes in DNA associated with a higher or lower risk of developing Alzheimer's.

Wide-scale screening has identified genetic regions and genes that appear to influence disease risk. Among them are variants of genes—CD33, BIN1, CR1, and MS4A6A—that encode proteins with various functions. For instance, CD33 and CR1 provide the genetic instructions for receptors on the cell surface that detect signals from other cells. These genes discovered by screening across populations have relatively modest effects on disease risk.

Researchers have also sequenced the genomes of thousands of people with Alzheimer's to look for rare variants that might exert a strong effect on disease risk. Several of these risk genes are expressed predominantly by microglia, the brain's major immune cells. In 2013 two studies identified a rare variant in TREM2, a gene encoding a receptor that traverses the cell membrane in microglia, as strongly increasing the risk of developing Alzheimer's.

The sequencing data revealed a variant that substituted an amino acid called histidine for arginine. This mutation was found to impair microglia's functioning and increase the risk of developing Alzheimer's roughly twofold to fourfold. Interestingly, like several of the other new risk-factor genes, TREM2 is expressed exclusively by microglia in the brain. These genetic clues suggested that microglia could actively contribute to the disease process, but how?

Surveillance Squad

Microglia are related to immune cells called macrophages that patrol the body to combat pathogens or help repair injured tissue. Researchers are learning that they are involved in everything from defense against infection to pruning excess synapses—the junctions where neurons meet—in the developing brain.

Under normal conditions, microglia have small cell bodies with branchlike protrusions that extend throughout brain tissue. The immune cells gobble up–or, more formally, phagocytose–unneeded synapses and debris, and they look for signs of injury or invasion by pathogens.

If injury does occur, the shape and function of microglia change. The cell bodies get larger, and the branches extending from them shorten and decrease in number. Microglia migrate to the site of an injury to initiate an inflammatory response. For decades researchers had observed microglia surrounding amyloid plaques. It was unknown, though, whether they helped to limit amyloid buildup or initiated toxic inflammation. The relation between microglia and tau also was not well understood.

Some studies have indicated that microglia act on neurons to damage axons and synapses, jamming signals transmitted along axons and resulting in an accumulation of tau in cells.

Other research shows that inflammatory proteins called cytokines that are secreted by microglia dramatically increase the destructive process of hyperphosphorylation. The discovery of genetic risk factors such as TREM2 and CD33 pointed to distinct molecules in microglia that could be involved in Alzheimer's. Researchers hope that understanding how these proteins function will provide insight into the broader role these cells play in the disease process.

Experimental mice are valuable tools for studying how genetic factors can influence the kinds of brain changes seen in human Alzheimer's dementia. So far there are few experimental animals that reproduce all aspects of Alzheimer's (for example, a mouse with amyloid-plaque buildup followed by the spread of pathological tau and accompanying neurodegeneration). But researchers have created several dozen "models"–genetically engineered mice that develop either amyloid plaque or tau.

By crossing these transgenic mice with mice engineered to express alterations in Alzheimer's risk genes, researchers can determine how a gene variant influences different aspects of

Alzheimer's-like pathology. For example, two decades ago amyloid mouse models engineered to express human APOE4 protein were shown to develop more amyloid plaques than mice with the APOE3 or APOE2 gene variants. In recent years researchers have assessed the role of the human TREM2 protein in Alzheimer's by deleting the Trem2 gene in mouse models of amyloid pathology. Several laboratories consistently identified a dramatic reduction in the number of microglia surrounding amyloid plaques in such mice.

A series of studies from the lab of Marco Colonna at Washington University in St. Louis found that in mice without the Trem2 gene, microglia were unable to properly ramp up their metabolism. When near amyloid plaques, they did not produce sufficient adenosine triphosphate, or ATP, a molecule that fuels cellular activity. Starved of energy, the cells were unable to surround amyloid plaques. Researchers then saw an increase in swollen, injured axons, known as dystrophic neurites, caused by damage from amyloid.

These key observations–fewer microglia surrounding plaques and increased damage to axons–were also seen in postmortem brain sections from people with Alzheimer's who had a rare mutation in the TREM2 gene known as R47H, the one that had been discovered in 2013. This finding boosted the confidence that the observations in mice could be relevant to how TREM2 works in humans. In addition, work by Jaime Grutzendler's group at Yale University showed that the fewer microglia that surrounded a plaque, the more damaged the nearby axons were.

That study provided further evidence of the potential role of microglia in protecting against amyloid's toxic effects in local areas around plaques. It also showed that microglia interact with the ends of tiny amyloid fibers, potentially halting their growth or shielding the surrounding neurons from amyloid's ill effects.

Toxic Seed

If microglia protect axons from amyloid plaque damage, might they also safeguard against tau pathology? If so, dangerous TREM2 mutations such as R47H might exacerbate Alzheimer's pathology by making it easier for neuritic plaque tau to develop near amyloid plaques. Testing this hypothesis remains challenging, but some clues have come from research exploring how tau pathology is able to spread similarly to prions, the proteins that characterize diseases such as Creutzfeldt-Jakob disease, one form of which is associated with "mad cow" disease.

Over the past decade or so researchers have found that tau and amyloid fold up into aberrant shapes similar to a prionlike "seed" that then causes normally structured forms of the proteins to misfold as well. In this manner, pathological tau can propagate to connected brain regions as Alzheimer's progresses. A series of papers by Virginia Man-Yee Lee's lab at the University of Pennsylvania showed that injecting normal mouse brains with aggregated tau seeds isolated from brains with Alzheimer's pathology resulted in the misfolding of mouse tau into neurofibrillary tangles. Mice that already had amyloid pathology developed neuritic plaque tau, the axon-damaging form of the protein. The latter process resembles the chain of events in Alzheimer's. Although the mice did not develop significant neurodegeneration, the "seeding" approach provided a reliable method to study both amyloid and tau pathology.

When it is not contributing to Alzheimer's pathology, tau is normally located in the axons of neurons, where it helps to stabilize structural proteins called microtubules that aid in the transport of cellular materials from one part of a neuron to another. Lee's team found that tau in swollen axons near amyloid plaques became disengaged from microtubules, leaving it potentially more prone to contortion. In essence, these damaged axons turned into fertile soil in which pathological tau seeds in the surrounding amyloid-laden cortex could take root.

Because the detrimental R47H-mutant type of TREM2 protein on microglia increases axon damage, we reasoned that the more common TREM2 form might help the immune cells shield axons near amyloid plaque, preventing tau seeds from spurring further tau accumulation or invading other areas of the cortex. In a study led by Cheryl Leyns and Maud Gratuze, then members of our lab, we injected tau seeds from an Alzheimer's brain into mouse models with and without genes expressing functional TREM2 protein and found that mice without the protein developed far more neuritic plaque tau in the swollen axons. That damage spread to other regions in the brain through networks of connected neurons.

We also used mouse models developed by Colonna that expressed either normal human TREM2 or the R47H form. Again, amyloid mouse models with the R47H variant developed more neuritic plaque tau pathology near amyloid plaques when injected with tau seeds. To confirm the findings from mouse models, we also examined human brains and found that people with Alzheimer's-associated TREM2 variants had more neuritic plaque tau. From these observations, we concluded that normal TREM2 and perhaps microglia in general protect against amyloid- induced seeding and spreading of tau throughout the brain.

Microglia seem to be protective against the spread of tau pathology in the amyloid-laden cortex typical of the first phase of Alzheimer's. But are they still protective once neurofibrillary tangles develop in the cortex and neurodegeneration begins during the symptomatic phase of the disease? Two influential studies–one from Ido Amit's lab at the Weizmann Institute of Science in Rehovot, Israel, and the other from Oleg Butovsky of Brigham and Women's Hospital and his colleagues–looked at changes in the activity of microglial genes in mouse models of different neurodegenerative diseases and identified remarkable similarities in how those genes are activated.

They found that microglia in mouse brains with neurodegenerative injuries similar to those that occur with tau pathology switched on diverse genes, many of which encode proteins for degrading unwanted materials in the cell. Microglia at this point strongly increased expression of a mouse version of the APOE4 risk gene. It seems then that both APOE and TREM2 play key roles in determining whether a microglial response is activated when neurons start to die and symptoms first appear.

That discovery led us to cross mice expressing different versions of human APOE with a mouse model that develops both tau pathology and severe neurodegeneration. In a study led by Yang Shi at our lab at Washington University in St. Louis, we found that a tau mouse model that expressed APOE4 had far more neurodegeneration and more advanced tau pathology than mice with APOE3 or APOE2. Next we assessed cell death in people with Alzheimer's or other neurodegenerative diseases with large accumulations of tau. We found that APOE4 carriers suffered greater damage in the brain than those who carried other alleles.

Additionally, Alzheimer's patients who were APOE4 carriers declined faster than those who were not. This came as a surprise to us and other researchers because for many years, it had been thought that the primary effect of APOE4 was the accumulation of large amounts of amyloid. These studies, however, pointed to a role for APOE4 not only in regulating amyloid pathology but also in dictating how fast neurons die in response to tau pathology. This implies that the "Alzheimer's gene," as APOE4 is known, influences not only amyloid deposition but also neurological damage because of tau accumulation, the two major disease stages.

The expanding understanding of APOE4 led to the next mouse experiment. We found that deletion of the mouse version of the APOE gene was strongly protective against neurodegeneration and delayed the progression of tau pathology—and, more important, the brain damage caused by tau buildup. If deletion of the APOE gene is neuroprotective in mouse models, then perhaps decreasing APOE levels in the human brain would slow down neurodegeneration, particularly in people carrying the APOE4 variant.

In another experiment, we used the tau mouse model, which also expressed human APOE4, to test whether reducing levels of the apolipoprotein variant would protect against neurodegeneration. We collaborated with Ionis Pharmaceuticals to use antisense oligonucleotides, short stretches of modified DNA that degrade messenger RNA (the molecular instructions for a cell to make a specific protein) to reduce the amount of APOE4 in the mice's brains by half. We found that lowering APOE4 levels when tau pathology was starting to take hold preserved neurons and diminished inflammation and microglial activation in the mice's brains.

An emerging picture suggests that microglia play two different roles during the progression of Alzheimer's dementia. In mouse models of amyloid pathology, increased microglial activity around plaques appears to protect the brain. In mice with tau pathology, aberrant tau strongly increases the expression of microglial genes associated with neurodegeneration, and APOE4 seems to further inflame the brain. All of this indicates a strong immune response by microglia to tau pathology that correlates with increased damage, not protection of the brain.

Of course, correlations do not equal causation, and at that point in our research it was unclear whether the strong immune response seen in tau models that expressed APOE4 was driving the degeneration or was simply a response to it. We next asked whether the loss of TREM2, the receptor on the surface of microglia, would increase neurodegeneration and inflammation in the brain. It would not have been entirely surprising if microglia helped to protect neurons, even at that relatively late stage of the disease.

Again, an experiment lowering gene activity was in store. Knocking out TREM2 in tau mouse models decreased the microglial response and diminished neurodegeneration levels. This finding suggested that reducing microglial activity resulted in less damage and brain atrophy from tau pathology.

A Double-Edged Sword

More evidence implicating microglia as drivers of the neuron loss that leads to cognitive decline later in the disease process came from two 2019 studies. Giving mice a drug that blocked the critical protein colony-stimulating factor 1, which microglia need to survive, was shown to remove around 90 percent of microglia in the brain. In tau mouse models, mice that received the drug exhibited dramatically reduced tau pathology and neurodegeneration, indicating that microglia are required for tau-dependent neurodegeneration. These findings demonstrate that TREM2 signaling appears to produce paradoxical effects—either protective or detrimental—depending on the stage of disease progression.

From this research, it seems likely that TREM2 signaling during the presymptomatic and possibly the early symptomatic phases of Alzheimer's, when amyloid accumulates, helps to reduce the amount of damage amyloid can inflict on nearby axons and synapses. It also impedes the advance of tau through the cortex. Once tau pathology is clearly established, however, microglia may drive synapse loss and the death of neurons.

Assuming that the damaging effect of microglia in mouse models of tau pathology holds true in human Alzheimer's—still a big assumption—targeting microglia might be a viable treatment strategy. It might be best to promote microglial activation, particularly around amyloid plaques, in the presymptomatic and early symptomatic phases of the illness. Conversely, in more advanced stages of tau pathology, decreasing the microglia response might slow neurodegeneration, as well as the rate of cognitive decline.

Perhaps as we learn more about how microglia behave in response to amyloid and tau pathology, new targets can be identified for the development of therapies to treat this devastating disease. A human clinical trial is currently testing whether TREM2 activation can slow the course of early-stage Alzheimer's, and multiple other microglia-targeted therapies are entering drug-development pipelines. If these approaches prove successful, it may turn out to be the third, overlooked finding in Alzheimer's famous autopsy—after the better-known plaques and tangles—that proves instrumental in decreasing the terrible impact on patients' brains.

About the Authors

Jason Ulrich is an associate professor of neurology at Washington University in St. Louis.

David M. Holtzman is professor and chair of neurology, scientific director of the Hope Center for Neurological Disorders at Washington University in St. Louis and associate director of the Knight Alzheimer's Disease Research Center. He is co-founder of C2N Diagnostics and has consulting arrangements with and research grants from various other companies.

Section 4: Hacking COVID: The Search for a Vaccine

A Guide to the SARS-CoV-2 Coronavirus

By Mark Fischetti, Veronica Falconieri Hays, Britt Glaunsinger, Jen Christiansen

Even though mysteries remain about COVID-19 and the novel coronavirus that causes the disease, scientists have generated an incredible amount of detailed knowledge about how the virus works and how we can stop it.

Thousands of different coronaviruses inhabit the planet. Four of them are responsible for many of our common colds. Two others already triggered alarming outbreaks of disease: in 2002 a coronavirus caused severe acute respiratory syndrome, which killed more than 770 people worldwide, and in 2012 a different strain started Middle East respiratory syndrome, taking more than 800 lives. SARS burned out within a year; MERS still lingers.

SARS-CoV-2 has created a far deadlier pandemic, in part because it spreads rapidly and in part because once it infects a person it can lie undetected for a long time. An individual infected with the 2002 SARS coronavirus did not transmit it until 24 to 36 hours after displaying symptoms such as fever and dry cough; people feeling ill would naturally isolate themselves, or be diagnosed by doctors, before they made others sick. But people with COVID can transmit the virus before they show clear symptoms, or they may have no symptoms at all.

Scientists, working intensely, have invented novel vaccines in record time that provide excellent protection against the disease. They have also created drugs that lessen infection and complications.

Virus Invasion and Immune Response

A SARS-CoV-2 particle enters a person's nose or mouth and floats in the airway and lungs until it brushes against a cell that has an ACE2 receptor on the surface. The virus binds to that cell, slips inside, and uses the cell's machinery to make numerous copies of itself. They break out, leaving the cell for dead, and penetrate many other cells. Infected cells send out alarms to the immune system to try to neutralize or kill the pathogens, but the viruses can prevent or intercept the signals, buying time to replicate widely before a person shows symptoms. Vulnerable receptors are also found on other types of cells in the kidney, heart, and gut.

Drug and Vaccine Intervention

Commercial, government, and university scientists have developed vaccines against COVID in record time, and the products have saved millions of lives. The experts have also devised drugs to reduce disease complications. Most drugs do not destroy the virus directly but interfere with it enough to allow the body's immune system to clear the infection. Drugs generally do one of three things: stop a virus from attaching to a cell, prevent a virus from reproducing if it does invade a cell, or dampen an overreaction by the immune system, which can cause severe symptoms.

Mutations and Variants

The SARS-CoV-2 genome is a strand of RNA that is about 29,900 bases long–near the limit for RNA viruses. Influenza has about 13,500 bases, and the rhinoviruses that cause common colds have about 8,000. (A base, also called a nucleotide, is a building block of RNA and DNA.) When viruses copy their genome, many accidental errors, called mutations, can occur. As they accumulate, they can lead to variant viruses that have new ways to infect us. The major SARS-CoV-2 variants thus far, after the initial "Alpha" virus, include Gamma, Delta, Mu, and Omicron.

About the Authors

Mark Fischetti is a senior editor at Scientific American. *He covers all aspects of sustainability.*

Veronica Falconieri Hays, M.A., C.M.I., is a Certified Medical Illustrator based in the Washington, DC area specializing in medical, molecular, cellular, and biological visualization, including both still media and animation.

Britt Glaunsinger is a molecular virologist at the University of California, Berkeley, and the Howard Hughes Medical Institute.

Jen Christiansen is senior graphics editor at Scientific American.

What Immunity to COVID-19 Really Means

By Stacey McKenna

The U.S. Food and Drug Administration recently granted an "emergency use authorization" of a blood test for antibodies against SARS-CoV-2, the novel coronavirus that causes COVID-19. It is the first such test to receive approval for the U.S. market. And it comes at a time when health experts and leaders are embracing immunity as a potential end point to the pandemic. In Colorado, a company that makes a coronavirus antibody test has donated kits to the state's San Miguel County so that everyone there can be tested if they want to. And in Italy, politicians want to use antibody status to determine which people will get "back to work" passes.

Several ambitious surveys to test for these antibodies have now been launched around the globe. The World Health Organization's Solidarity II study will pool antibody data from more than half a dozen countries. In the U.S., a collaborative multiyear project aims to provide a picture of nationwide antibody prevalence. Its first phase is already collecting samples from blood donors in six major urban areas, including New York City, Seattle, and Minneapolis. And the effort will evolve into three national surveys of donors, supported by the Centers for Disease Control and Prevention and conducted this fall and in the fall of 2021.

Unlike diagnostic tests, which are used to confirm the presence and sometimes load, or amount, of the virus, antibody tests help determine whether or not someone was previously infected–even if that person never showed symptoms. Widespread use of such assays could give scientists greater insight into how deadly the virus is and how widely it has spread throughout the population.

It is less clear what those antibody tests mean for real life, however, because immunity functions on a continuum. With some pathogens, such as the varicella-zoster virus (which causes chicken pox), infection confers near-universal, long-lasting resistance. Natural infection with *Clostridium tetani*, the bacterium that causes tetanus, on the other hand, offers no protection—and even people getting vaccinated for it require regular booster shots. On the extreme end of this spectrum, individuals infected with HIV often have large amounts of antibodies that do nothing to prevent or clear the disease.

At this early stage of understanding the new coronavirus, it is unclear where COVID-19 falls on the immunity spectrum. Although most people with SARS-CoV-2 seem to produce antibodies, "we simply don't know yet what it takes to be effectively protected from this infection," says Dawn Bowdish, a professor of pathology and molecular medicine and Canada Research Chair in Aging and Immunity at McMaster University in Ontario. Researchers are scrambling to answer two questions: How long do SARS-CoV-2 antibodies stick around? And do they protect against reinfection?

Early on, some people—most notably U.K. Prime Minister Boris Johnson (who has the virus and is currently in intensive care) and his government's scientific adviser Patrick Vallance—touted hopes that herd immunity could be an eventual means for ending the pandemic. And although it appears that recovered COVID-19 patients have antibodies for at least two weeks, long-term data are still lacking. So many scientists are looking to other coronaviruses for answers.

Immunity to seasonal coronaviruses (such as those that cause common colds), for example, starts declining a couple of weeks after infection. And within a year, some people are vulnerable to reinfection. That observation is disconcerting when experts say it is unlikely we will have a vaccine for COVID-19 within 18 months. But studies of SARS-CoV—the virus that causes severe acute respiratory syndrome, or SARS, which shares a considerable amount of its genetic material with SARS-CoV-2—are more promising. Antibody testing shows SARS-CoV immunity peaks at around four months and offers protection for roughly two to three years. As Preeti Malani, chief health officer and a professor of medicine at the University of Michigan, said in a video interview with *JAMA* Editor in Chief

Howard Bauchner,this period presents “a pretty good time line for thinking about vaccines and therapeutics” for COVID-19.

Even if the antibodies stick around in the body, however, it is not yet certain that they will prevent future infection. What we want, Bowdish says, are neutralizing antibodies. These are the proteins that reduce and prevent infection by binding to the part of a virus that connects to and “unlocks” host cells. They are relatively easy to detect, and they are far easier for vaccine developers to generate than the alternative: the immune system’s T cells. In contrast, nonneutralizing antibodies still recognize parts of the pathogen, but they do not bind effectively and so do not prevent it from invading cells.

“If humans naturally make neutralizing antibodies [against SARS-CoV-2], then all we have to do is figure out what [sites they are] binding on the virus and really target that one little piece of protein, and that’s our magic bullet,” Bowdish says. For SARS-CoV-2, that target site is most likely on the so-called receptor-binding domain of its spike glycoprotein—a protein attached to a sugar that the virus uses to enter cells. But, Bowdish says, this spot may present a challenge because human immune systems are not very good at making antibodies against sugar-coated substances.

Nevertheless, a few small studies of cells in laboratory dishes suggest that SARS-CoV-2 infection triggers the production of neutralizing antibodies. And animal studies indicate such antibodies do prevent reinfection, at least for a couple of weeks. Furthermore, because some antibodies seem to recognize and react to the spike proteins on multiple coronaviruses, including SARS-CoV and MERS-CoV (the virus that causes Middle East respiratory syndrome, or MERS), researchers can build on knowledge learned from previous outbreaks.

Research on real-life immunity to SARS-CoV-2 is in its preliminary stages, and uncertainties remain. One study found no correlation between viral load and antibody presence, leading the authors to question the antibodies’ actual role in clearing the virus in humans. In addition, peer-reviewed research on SARS-CoV and preprint studies on SARS-CoV-2 report that some nonneutralizing coronavirus antibodies might trigger a harmful immune response upon reinfection with those pathogens or cross infection with other coronaviruses. Thus, while much of the emerging research is promising, Bowdish cautions against using antibody testing to drive policy until researchers know the proportion of COVID-19 survivors who are producing neutralizing antibodies.

In an ideal world, SARS-CoV-2 immunity would resemble that acquired by children who get chicken pox. Early research suggests we are in for a much more complex scenario but one that time and unprecedented global cooperation might be able to untangle. Eventually antibody tests could be the key to getting our lives and economies back on track. For now, they promise to give experts, officials, and citizens a clearer picture of the pandemic.

About the Author

Stacey McKenna is a medical anthropologist and freelance journalist who writes about science, travel, and all things equine.

COVID-19 Vaccine Developers Search for Antibodies That 'First Do No Harm'

By Esther Landhuis

The coronavirus pandemic has provided the world with a quick study in the intricacies of immunology. "Herd immunity" and "serological tests" have become household terms. Front and center among these concepts are antibodies. These immune proteins typically emerge during the second or third week after an infection, glomming onto invaders and preventing them from sneaking into human cells. If antibodies targeting a particular virus turn up in a blood sample, their appearance provides confirmation of an immune response that may protect against reinfection.

Eliciting the right antibodies to disarm SARS-CoV-2, the virus responsible for the current pandemic, is the goal of dozens of vaccine developers, several of which have already launched human trials in record time. But public health officials and scientists caution against moving too quickly. In rare instances, these immune defenders can exacerbate disease rather than guard against it.

That concern has not yet materialized in the early stages of making a COVID-19 vaccine. Yet based on research related to past coronavirus outbreaks, vaccine manufacturers do not view the hurdle as purely theoretical.

Typically SARS-CoV-2 and the earlier related coronavirus SARS-CoV make their way into cells through a docking site: a cell-surface receptor called ACE2. Vaccines that provide the sought-after immunization make "neutralizing" antibodies against viral proteins, blocking the pathogen's entrance through the ACE2 portal.

But just because an antibody can keep a virus from entering cells in a lab dish does not necessarily mean it will behave that way in the body, says Akiko Iwasaki, an immunologist at Yale University. In scenarios she describes in a recent Nature Reviews Immunology commentary, antibodies may occasionally help a virus invade and thwart immune cells that would normally engulf and help clear the pathogen.

If some of the antibodies produced do not bind to the virus well enough–or are not present in the right concentration–they can latch onto it and exacerbate disease through a process known as antibody-dependent enhancement (ADE). In ADE, antibody-coated viruses gain a "backdoor" entry through antibody receptors on macrophages and other members of the cellular cleanup crew–in essence, disabling the very cells that would have chopped up those viruses and chemically disposed of them. In some cases, this process can trigger a harmful inflammatory response.

Indeed, it seems that some pathogens, including coronaviruses, have "found a way to use the antibody as a Trojan horse" to infect disease-fighting cells," Iwasaki says. Her lab is working to understand the types of immune responses that help people recover from COVID-19 versus those that contribute to disease.

Through ADE, Iwasaki suggests, the virus can initiate an overproduction of inflammatory signaling proteins called cytokines, leading to "cytokine storms" that can promote acute respiratory distress syndrome and damage lung tissue. Similar problems can also be unleashed in some COVID-19 patients by other immune cells called neutrophils.

Scientists are not yet sure if ADE actually promotes cytokine storms or immune-related tissue damage in COVID-19. They are connecting hypothetical dots based on past studies of experimental vaccines for previous outbreaks of severe acute respiratory syndrome (SARS) and Middle East respiratory syndrome (MERS), in which some immunized animals developed more severe disease. Plus, earlier work by Iwasaki and others suggests that pathogens entering cells through the back door get shunted to different cellular compartments that are rich in receptors that sense microbial threats and release molecules linked to cytokine storms. "That's a well-known fact," Iwasaki says. "Why wouldn't SARS-CoV-2 also be recognized this way?"

Some research from earlier coronavirus outbreaks does, in fact, lend support to the idea that antibodies could trigger inflammatory pathology by co-opting macrophages. In an analysis of monkeys published last year in JCI Insight, researchers in China showed that SARS-CoV antibodies from serum in vaccinated animals were sufficient to trigger lung damage in a set of unvaccinated ones. The transferred antibodies worsened disease and seemed to switch lung macrophages from a protective to a pathogenic state, as judged by an examination of the immune cells' genetic activity.

ADE has cropped up as a suspected problem for other vaccines. Certain dengue and respiratory syncytial virus vaccines have provoked severe immune reactions. Antibodies could be one of the initiators, but vaccine scientists say immune-related tissue damage is a bigger potential concern. Liver and lung damage caused by an inflammatory reaction has occurred in animals infected with the SARS virus after vaccination. But ADE as a mechanism was documented in lab dish experiments, so the phenomenon "is a bit more theoretical," says Peter Hotez, co-director of the Texas Children's Hospital Center for Vaccine Development, which is building on its SARS vaccine work to create a COVID-19 vaccine.

While it is possible that suboptimal antibodies could lead to inflammation and tissue damage, he says these problems could also result from the aberrant activity of T cells, which serve as another virus fighter in the immune system's arsenal. A study published on May 14 in Cell suggests SARS-CoV-2-specific T cells, when functioning normally, may help people combat COVID-19.

Scientists are well aware of the potential danger of ADE. It is "something which may happen," says Paul Henri Lambert, a vaccine scientist at the University of Geneva and a consultant at the Coalition for Epidemic Preparedness Innovations (CEPI). "But at this stage, we do not have any evidence that this is a problem for vaccines against SARS-CoV-2."

Moderna, a Massachusetts biotech company that announced preliminary findings from an early-stage clinical trial of its RNA-based

COVID-19 vaccine last week, has found no serious health problems in study participants. Another COVID-19 vaccine that was tested in an early-stage trial in China appeared to be safe and produced neutralizing antibodies in some of the study's 108 participants, according to a May 22 study in the *Lancet*.

Several additional COVID-19 vaccines have been tested in nonhuman primates. One was made from an inactivated virus by researchers in China, who reported on May 6 that the highest dose gave protection. The team found no evidence for disease enhancement in four monkeys analyzed seven days after they were infected with SARS-CoV-2. A non-peer-reviewed paper on a second vaccine, developed using the SARS-CoV-2 protein responsible for viral entry into host cells, was posted on the preprint server bioRxiv on May 13. It also showed no signs of enhanced disease. And in a May 20 study of macaques immunized with another type of candidate (a DNA vaccine), scientists reported that they "did not observe enhanced clinical disease even with the suboptimal vaccine constructs that failed to protect."

Stanley Perlman, a physician and viral immunologist at the University of Iowa, has participated in COVID-19 vaccine committees set up by both the National Institutes of Health and the World Health Organization. These committees have thoroughly discussed possible risks posed by ADE, he says. But given the urgency of the pandemic, Perlman adds, "people say, we've got to get a vaccine yesterday. And on the other hand, you have people saying, 'Oh no, we have to be really careful.' How to balance this? We can't open up the country until we have a vaccine, until we have herd immunity. So it becomes a difficult question: What's the most correct course of action?"

The real question is whether COVID-19 vaccines will cause ADE when they are given to hundreds of thousands of people. This concern is shared by researchers testing if blood plasma from recovered patients can safely treat people hospitalized with the disease. ADE has not been reported thus far in a study of 5,000 patients given this convalescent plasma nationwide, which was posted on May 14 on the preprint server medRxiv.

Analyses of immune responses in early-stage clinical trial volunteers and nonhuman primates studied before moving on to the next phase of a given investigation should be able to identify vaccines at potential risk for immune enhancement, Lambert says. Hotez thinks it will be important to watch for ADE and damaging inflammatory reactions when immunizing study participants in areas where the virus is spreading. "If you're going to see a problem, that's where you would see it," he says. "In individuals who are vaccinated and then exposed to the virus, you would want to monitor for liver and lung function to make sure there's no worsening."

Beyond vaccines, ADE could influence other aspects of the immune response to SARS-CoV-2. Jorge Caballero, a Stanford University anesthesiologist who organizes data and engineering support for COVID-19 surveillance testing, wonders if the process could underlie other disease manifestations, including "COVID toes," respiratory distress linked to lung pathology, and a mysterious inflammatory condition striking some kids with the disease. Emerging data "suggest that the common link–Occam's razor, if you will–may be a little understood phenomenon known as antibody-dependent enhancement," he says.

About the Author

Esther Landhuis is a freelance science and health journalist based in the San Francisco Bay Area.

Fast-Track Drugs

By Michael Waldholz

Mark Denison began hunting for a drug to treat COVID-19 almost a decade before the contagion, driven by a novel coronavirus, devastated the world this year. Denison is not a prophet, but he is a virologist and an expert on the often deadly coronavirus family, members of which also caused the SARS outbreak in 2002 and the MERS eruption in 2012. It is a big viral group, and "we were pretty certain another one would soon emerge," says Denison, who directs the division of pediatric infectious diseases at Vanderbilt University Medical Center.

A virus is an unusual beast. Essentially it is a cluster of genetic material that integrates itself into a cell and takes over some of the cell's molecular machinery, using it to assemble an army of viral copies. Those clones burst out of the cell, destroying it, and go on to infect nearby cells. Viruses are hard to kill off completely because of their cellular integration–they hide within their hosts. And they have explosive reproductive rates. Because total eradication is so hard, antiviral drugs instead aim to limit replication to low levels that cannot hurt the body.

In 2013 Denison and Ralph Baric, a coronavirus researcher at the University of North Carolina at Chapel Hill, identified a vulnerable site on a protein common to all coronaviruses they had examined, a spot that is key to the microbe's ability to make copies of itself. If that ability is hindered, a coronavirus cannot cause widespread infection. Four years later researchers in the two laboratories spotted a compound that acted on this protein site. It was sitting, unused, in a large library of antiviral compounds created by the biotech giant Gilead Biosciences. The scientists got a sample and, in test tube and animal experiments, showed that the drug, called remdesivir, shut down the replicating machinery of several coronavirus variants.

So in early January, when the alarms rang about SARS-CoV-2, Denison and Baric alerted colleagues at Gilead that they were sitting on a potential treatment. Largely because of its activity against other coronavirus strains in Denison and Baric's animal studies, remdesivir was made available to patients for "compassionate use" in January. By March, Gilead had rushed the compound into two human trials, planning to test the drug's safety and most effective doses on about 1,000 ill patients over several months; health authorities in China began two similar trials. While that was happening, Denison, Baric and a group of their colleagues at Emory University identified still another compound, called EIDD-2801, that hits the same viral vulnerability. In early April they published results showing that in mice, the new substance helped breathing and reduced the amount of many coronaviruses. In test-tube experiments with human lung cells, it drastically hindered SARS-CoV-2.

Several labs around the world, like Denison's and Baric's, have logged years of experience poking about the inner workings of coronaviruses because of SARS and MERS. By the time the new coronavirus was genetically sequenced and its structure revealed, scientists already had identified the enzymes and proteins that most coronaviruses use to spread from one infected human cell to another and also understood that the body could create an overly aggressive inflammatory response when the virus infected lung airway cells.

Because of this work, three main strategies for impeding the virus have emerged as the labs have turned to the current threat. One strategy is to find compounds like remdesivir and EIDD-2801 that gum up the virus's reproductive machinery when it enters a target cell. A second is to block the virus, like a bouncer outside a bar, from entering and infecting those cells in the first place. The third approach is to muffle the immune system's dangerously overactive response, a "cytokine storm" that can drown a victim in a mass of congestion and dying airway cells.

To find these drugs, researchers have turned to the Food and Drug Administration's list of some 20,000 compounds approved for human use and crawled through drug patent applications looking for compounds with promising mechanisms of action. The goal has been to find drugs that have been at least partly developed, avoiding years of making therapeutic molecules from scratch. The Milken Institute, a health advocacy think tank, counted 133 experimental COVID-19 treatments in mid-April. About 49 of these therapies are being rushed into clinical trials. Their effectiveness in people is not yet known, and scientists caution that such drugs, like other antivirals, are unlikely to be cures. But they could reduce symptoms enough to give patients' immune systems a chance to beat the virus on their own.

Copy Stoppers

All coronaviruses use the same mechanism to reproduce, which involves an enzyme called viral RNA polymerase, so Baric says that was an obvious target. The polymerase makes lots of mistakes as it copies the virus, and it relies on another enzyme, known as an exonuclease, to "proofread" and fix them. Remdesivir appears to disable the proofreading enzyme. Then the virus's copying factory becomes sloppy and produces fewer new viruses.

EIDD-2801, the compound with promising animal and test-tube results reported in early April, aims at the same viral enzyme. But unlike remdesivir, which much be given intravenously, EIDD-2801 can be taken as a pill. For this reason, Baric and other researchers investigating EIDD-2801, including George Painter, a professor of pharmacology and president of the Emory Institute for Drug Development, which first produced the drug, suspect it may end up being more widely used than remdesivir.

In 2018 Painter and his colleagues identified EIDD-2801's activity during a search for a universal influenza medicine. When SARS-CoV-2 emerged, Painter's group immediately shifted focus.

EIDD-2801, like remdesivir, inhibits the coronavirus's self-copying operations, but it also works against virus variants with a mutation that made them resistant to the Gilead drug. In addition, EIDD-2801 is effective against a host of other RNA viruses, so it could serve as a multipurpose antiviral, much as some antibiotics can work against a wide variety of bacteria. For COVID-19, says Wayne Holman, co-founder of Miami-based Ridgeback Biotherapeutics, which has licensed the drug and is planning clinical trials, the goal is to have a pill that can be taken by patients at home early in the course of the disease to prevent it from progressing.

Blocking Infection

To stop SARS-CoV-2 from penetrating cells in the first place, scientists are trying to develop antibodies that lock onto the viral protein that facilitates cell entry, a part of the virus known as the spike. Some of these neutralizing antibodies, made of a protein called immunoglobulin, may come from the blood of patients who have already cleared the virus. Several medical centers, including Johns Hopkins Hospital and the Mayo Clinic, are harvesting blood plasma from survivors and screening it for antibodies. In a technique known as convalescent therapy, doctors then transfuse it into hospitalized patients with life-threatening acute respiratory distress. Early studies of a few such patients suggest the approach may work–some patients' symptoms improved, and levels of the virus in their bodies dropped–but the work is very preliminary.

Takeda Pharmaceuticals, a Japanese firm, is also collecting plasma from recovered COVID-19 patients to identify antibodies. In that plasma, the company is identifying antibodies that show the most activity against SARS-CoV-2. Using these antibodies as a template, the Takeda researchers plan to synthesize a batch of even more active versions to create a potent cocktail of infection inhibitors, says Chris Morabito, head of research and development of plasma-derived therapies. The therapy–TAK-888–might enter clinical trials by year's end, Morabito says; the number "888" represents "triple fortune" in Chinese. Several other drugmakers, including Regeneron and Vir Biotechnology, are generating their own therapeutic antibodies and say they will also be tested in patients this year.

Another blockade strategy focuses on the cellular docking site that the virus uses. Josef Penninger, a molecular biologist at the University of British Columbia in Vancouver and founder of drug company Apeiron Biologics, is trying to lure the virus away from a chemical receptor called ACE2 in the outer wall of lung cells. The coronavirus spike protein binds to this receptor. Several years ago Penninger's lab synthesized a decoy version of ACE2. In test-tube experiments, the scientists found the synthetic molecule–APN01–attracted coronaviruses away from real human airway cells. The virus locked onto the decoy and was marooned there. "We are blocking the door for the virus and, at the same time, protecting tissues," Penninger says. Apeiron is planning clinical trials later this year for APN01, which must be administered in the hospital as an infusion to sick patients.

Overreactions

In the sickest COVID-19 patients, a mass of mucuslike fluid accumulates in the lungs, preventing cells from absorbing oxygen. These are the patients that need ventilators. The fluid buildup is the result of an overactive immune response that involves a signaling chemical called interleukin-6 (IL-6). Biotech companies, including Regeneron and Genentech, have manufactured synthetic antibodies that can bind to IL-6 and mute the call to action that it sends out.

Northwell Health, a large system of 23 hospitals based in Long Island, N.Y., is one of more than a dozen centers participating in clinical trials of the IL-6 blockers, says Kevin Tracey, chief executive of the Feinstein Institutes for Medical Research, which is running the trials at Northwell sites. "The hospitals are being inundated with very sick patients suffering from serious pneumonia and acute respiratory distress," Tracey says. "The IL-6 drugs have a plausible mechanism of action. I'm optimistic they'll work."

None of these approaches are cures. Denison says the drugs under development may "reduce the severity" of an advanced COVID-19 episode, especially if they can be administered when initial symptoms–a mild cough, muscle aches, or slight fever–first arise. In a hopeful future, a combination of various therapies may be able to thwart the virus on several different fronts, the way a cocktail of antivirals can beat back an HIV/AIDS infection. By limiting symptoms, drugs may be able to keep some patients out of the hospital and keep hospitalized patients off of ventilators. They can serve as a bridge to survival as other scientists rush to develop the real virus slayer: a vaccine.

About the Author

Journalist Michael Waldholz led a team of reporters who were awarded a Pulitzer Prize in 1997 for their coverage of AIDS. He lives in New York State's Hudson Valley.

Section 5: Future Hacks: Learning from COVID

How Communication around COVID Fuels a Mistrust of Science

By Joseph V. Sakran, Kavita K. Patel

The highly contagious COVID Omicron variant is shattering new U.S. daily case records. With Omicron carrying a risk of breakthrough infection five times higher than that of the Delta variant, we are witnessing a significant impact on the American workforce in all sectors. The increase in cases among essential workers has sidelined many health care workers, resulted in thousands of holiday flights being canceled, and once again disrupted our supply chain.

In the meantime, the U.S. Centers for Disease Control and Prevention (CDC) is adding to the chaos in the way it changed its isolation recommendations. What originally was 10 days of isolation after initial contact with someone who tested positive for COVID has turned into five days of isolation, and upon reentry into civilization, five more days of wearing a mask. To complicate matters further, the CDC has also introduced an option to test out of isolation if a test is readily available (which in the United States is currently not the case).

These changes, which started as guidance focused on health care personnel before it was suggested to the general public, give reason to suspect the agency was motivated by pressure from the business community rather than consideration of the science. As recently reported, the CEO of Delta Air Lines sent a letter pressing the head of the CDC for such a move in order to preserve the airline's workforce. With such a shift from our top public health agency comes a palpable sense of frustration in the country, and the further eroding of public faith in science, the scientific process, and scientists themselves.

For us as physicians steeped in empirical evidence, to think that our health and the health of our patients potentially could be compromised because of business interests feels like a serious blow, undermining even our confidence in the agency.

But perhaps we all saw this coming.

Throughout the pandemic, we have seen how inconsistent messaging around COVID has fueled doubt around science, giving place to consistently messaged misinformation that has found its way into communities all across America. This has undermined our ability to implement data-driven policymaking.

Even before the pandemic, science has been under attack with debates over whether climate change is real, whether tobacco or vaping causes lung damage, whether guns are associated with gun violence, and whether mental illness is simply a chemical imbalance or more broadly related to a bio-psycho-social model.

We have seen anti-vaccine sentiment prevail after Andrew Wakefield's work linking autism to vaccines was published. Dozens of peer-reviewed studies have found exactly the opposite. Wakefield's paper was retracted, and he's been resoundingly discredited as a scientist, but the damage is done. Prior to COVID-19, we saw measles outbreaks reach their highest numbers since measles was all but eliminated. Why? Pockets of American communities, fearing autism, simply refused vaccination. Children died of a preventable disease.

As the pandemic continues, our public health agencies, starting at the very top, need to be reliable, evidence-driven, and consistent sources of information. But the CDC is not alone. Our top drug regulatory agency, the U.S. Food and Drug Administration (FDA), has shown inconsistency that not only affects the general public, but everyone who is involved in health care delivery.

Take Aduhelm, for instance. Several months prior to the approval of the Alzheimer's disease drug, a group of senior FDA officials agreed that there wasn't enough evidence for approval of the drug. The officials said the agency should require further evidence that the drug worked the way the company said it did prior to re-review or approval. This came as a blow to patients, clinicians, and researchers who were incredibly hopeful for a potential treatment of such a devastating disease that lacks therapeutic options.

Despite the setback, the scientific community agreed that further clinical work should be done. Shortly after the consensus decision by advisory members and senior scientists, the FDA controversially approved the drug with no additional clinical studies and zero acknowledgment of the lack of data behind the approval. After weeks of incredible backlash and the resignation of several key advisory members, then acting FDA commissioner Janet Woodcock made a 180-degree reversal that went from making statements expressing confidence in the agency's decision to then supporting an independent investigation that led to the approval of the drug.

That flip left the medical community dumbfounded over the decision to initially approve Aduhelm, which still defies explanation.

Scientists and health care professionals have long viewed institutions such as the CDC and FDA with respect. However, the mixed messages, and the doubt they have created in our minds signal a much deeper problem that will require innovative solutions.

We are entering the third year of an infectious disease war that has killed over 800,000 Americans. At the same time, many more Americans are dying from firearm injuries, drug overdoses, suicides, and delayed medical care. Health care professionals are physically and emotionally exhausted and have worked through some of the darkest periods of this pandemic–whether it's the lack of protective personal equipment (PPE), the personal sacrifice of their lives, or putting their families and loved ones at risk for contracting the virus.

Meanwhile, people are still not getting vaccinated, government leaders like U.S. Secretary of Defense Lloyd Austin are contracting breakthrough cases of COVID, and the American workforce is being crippled by the exponential uptick in positive cases.

It's clear that we are struggling to smother this fire. Part of our success in doing so rests in our ability to restore trust in our scientific institutions.

The leaders of government agencies and the public sector, including public and for-profit health care and research institutions, should create a rapid response system that evaluates the newest data around COVID and quickly provides feedback to best ensure the most consistent, evidence-based messaging is released to the health care workforce and the general public. Similar to the peer review process, elevating the evaluation of significant policies to a larger peer group is a strategy that may be useful.

It's also important to include frontline healthcare workers in these conversations. They are closest to the struggle and often know what the best solutions are.

As an important group of trusted professionals, public health practitioners, and scientific organizations must do a better job at communicating our message, especially during a crisis where the landscape is rapidly changing. All of us are prone to mistakes, and while no one expects any individual or organization to be perfect, setting consistent expectations during a public health crisis is critical. The strategy and approach in how we communicate the message, is just as important as having the right idea.

About the Authors

Joseph V. Sakran is an associate professor of surgery and nursing, and director of emergency general surgery, Johns Hopkins Hospital, and senior fellow, Satcher Health Leadership Institute. He holds M.D., M.P.H. and M.P.A. degrees.

Kavita K. Patel is a primary care physician at Mary's Center in Washington, D.C., and was previously a director of policy in the Obama White House. She holds M.D. and M.S.H.S. degrees.

The Vaccine Rollout Is Changing How We Think about Prescription Meds

By Mark Westall

America's successful COVID vaccine rollout is having profound short-term effects, leading more cities and states to reduce restrictions and reopen parts of their economies–and most recently, leading the CDC to relax its guidance on wearing masks. It's also likely to have lasting effects that could change how millions of people live their lives. One of those will be what prescription medicines people choose to take.

In a new survey, my company, M Booth Health, found that a seismic shift has already begun. People are changing the ways they talk to their doctors about all of their medicines, and in particular, which prescription medications they accept or reject.

With a historic pandemic bringing unprecedented upheaval to their lives, people have spent more time and energy learning about science and medicine. They've become more knowledgeable and empowered. This goes beyond just COVID; it extends into all of their medical needs.

The majority (57 percent) told us they are now more likely to read up on the science behind any vaccine or medication. Nearly as many (55 percent) said they'll ask their doctors about all their therapeutic options instead of accepting the first recommendation they receive.

The effects of this are difficult to overestimate. About half the U.S. population takes prescription drugs. More than 4 billion prescriptions are dispensed each year, topping half a trillion dollars in spending. So even slight changes in which medicines people select could affect millions of people and tens of millions of dollars.

The changes are being driven by a new way people are thinking about pharmaceutical companies. In the past, consumers have given little if any thought to which company is behind the vaccines and medicines they take. For example, although 55 percent of Americans had the latest flu vaccine, in our survey only 3 percent of consumers could name a company that manufactures a flu vaccine.

But the past year, which has included months of intense news coverage of COVID vaccines, has given pharmaceutical companies a new place top of mind. Ninety percent of the people we polled are now familiar with Pfizer, and 80 percent are familiar with Moderna. (The maker of the third vaccine available in the United States, Johnson & Johnson, had even higher name recall, but it was already widely known because of its consumer products.)

Consumers' heightened recognition of drug companies is not limited to the vaccine makers. People have read and learned more about others as well. Bayer, AstraZeneca (which made a vaccine available in some other countries), Merck, and Bristol Myers Squibb are now all familiar names to more than half of our respondents.

Most strikingly, consumers now prefer one brand over another. This begins with preferences for a vaccine, but it extends outward from there. In our poll, many respondents told us that going forward they'll prefer medicines from their favorite brands.

Nearly half (44 percent) of Americans plan to tell their doctor about personal preferences for medications manufactured by certain pharmaceutical companies. These figures are larger among younger people, suggesting that it's a wave of the future. More than half (52 percent) of Gen Z respondents said they will do so.

The biggest "winner" in this respect is Pfizer. When it comes to vaccines specifically, more than 70 percent of Americans prefer one by name: 36 percent prefer Pfizer–as many as Moderna (19 percent) and Johnson & Johnson (17 percent) combined.

Doctors say there is no "best" vaccine, and the CDC has no preference. Still, among most Americans, preferences and even a sense of "vaccine elitism"– the belief some people have that their vaccine choice is superior–have taken hold.

As a result of these changes, pharmaceutical companies are likely to put more efforts into reaching out to consumers directly.

Expect more marketing from these companies talking about the work they do and what they stand for.

Pharma executives are also likely to take on larger public profiles. Nearly half of our respondents (46 percent) said they want to hear more from pharmaceutical brand leaders.

One in three respondents told us they now think of pharmaceutical companies as being similar to household name brands like Nike and Amazon. This is a sea change–one with repercussions that could be felt for decades to come.

This is an opinion and analysis article

About the Author

Mark Westall is vice president, research and planning, for M Booth Health.

We Need a Universal Flu Vaccine before the Next Pandemic Strikes

By Catharine I. Paules, Anthony S. Fauci

This year the world will mark the 100th anniversary of one of the most devastating infectious disease events in recorded history: the 1918 influenza pandemic, which caused an estimated 50 million to 100 million deaths worldwide.

There were several reasons for the awful toll. First, most people likely had no preexisting immune protection to the brand-new strain that had emerged. Second, this particular virus may have been unusually lethal. Third, crowding and poor sanitation allowed for rampant disease transmission, especially in regions where access to health care was limited. And finally, antiviral drugs and flu vaccines were still decades in the future.

Over the past century we have made substantial advances in all these areas. But we are still unprepared for the inevitable appearance of a virus like the one that struck a century ago. Even an ordinary seasonal flu epidemic will still kill some 12,000 to 56,000 people every year in the U.S. alone. That is because seasonal viruses continually evolve, and although we update our vaccines frequently, they may be only 40 to 60 percent effective. Moreover, seasonal vaccines may provide little or no protection against pandemic flu. Pandemic viruses typically arise from a process referred to as an antigenic shift, in which the new virus acquires, usually from animal influenza viruses, one or more genes that are entirely novel (as seems to have happened in 1918, when all eight pandemic virus genes were novel).

In the years since 1918, three influenza pandemics associated with antigenic shifts occurred: in 1957, 1968, and 2009. In each of these instances, however, the new viruses emerged via the mixing of animal influenza virus genes with those of the 1918-descended viruses already circulating in the human population, which meant that many people were at least partially immune. That, plus lower viral pathogenicity and improvements in public health infrastructure and medical treatment, is what probably led to less catastrophic pandemics.

We must also tackle the issue of "prepandemic" influenza viruses–those that could potentially cause pandemics but that have not (yet) done so. Human infections with avian influenza viruses have occurred with increasing frequency over the past two decades. Prepandemic vaccines against various strains of H5N1 and H7N9 viruses have been developed and in some cases stockpiled; similar to seasonal influenza viruses, however, these avian strains are subject to antigenic drift within their avian hosts. Many of the H7N9 avian viruses that have jumped species from poultry to cause human infections in China in 2016 and 2017 have changed significantly from 2013 avian strains. As a result, the human immune responses elicited by a vaccine developed against the 2013 H7N9 virus may not be effective against 2017 strains.

The remarkable capacity of influenza viruses to undergo antigenic drift or shift to overcome and escape human population immunity leaves us vulnerable to a public health disaster potentially as serious as the 1918 pandemic. To meet this global health challenge, scientists are working to develop "universal influenza vaccines"–new types of inoculations that can provide protection not only against changing seasonal influenza viruses but also against the inevitable pandemic viruses that will emerge in the future.

Recently the National Institute of Allergy and Infectious Diseases convened a workshop with leading experts in the influenza field to address the need for better influenza vaccines. Among many obstacles to developing a universal vaccine, the most formidable is our incomplete understanding of the immune responses that protect people against influenza, including the role of immunity at mucosal surfaces.

One approach is to design a vaccine to generate antibody responses to parts of the virus that are common to all influenza strains and do not readily change by mutation. It is also crucial to clarify how other parts of the immune system work together with antibodies to protect against influenza. The hurdles in the development of such vaccines are daunting. But we are optimistic that we can apply existing tools and experimental strategies to meet the challenge. As we note the centennial of the 1918 flu pandemic, let us remind ourselves of the importance of this line of research in preventing a repeat of one of the most disastrous events in the history of global health.

About the Authors

Catharine I. Paules is a medical officer in the Office of the Director at the National Institute of Allergy and Infectious Diseases.

Anthony S. Fauci is director of the National Institute of Allergy and Infectious Diseases.

Contagions Worse Than COVID Will Prevail If Neglect of Global Public Health Continues

By the Editors of *Scientific American*

After Omicron comes pi in the Greek alphabet. And then rho, sigma, tau.... Before SARS-CoV-2 finishes its grand tour through the Greek alphabet, the global public health establishment should do what it should have done long before this coronavirus emerged. It must put in place the basic health systems needed to detect new outbreaks and deploy technologies that allow for vaccines and medicines to be manufactured and administered in low- and middle-income countries.

Because they have often refused to treat COVID as a common threat that demands a unified response, policy makers have yet to thwart the predations of a virus that, to channel the Greeks again, affects all (pan) people (demos). This myopia means that these mistakes could be repeated when a new pandemic arrives.

The next time could be worse. The National Academy of Medicine predicted in November 2021 that a flu epidemic akin to the one in 1918 and 1919 could prove more catastrophic than COVID-19. The preconditions for such a disaster are in place. A warming planet, megacities, mass migration, intercontinental travel, and habitat loss are among the reasons that infectious diseases, like intensifying typhoons and hurricanes, have become part of our lives.

Fast-tracked development of diagnostics, vaccines, monoclonal antibodies, and antiviral drugs marks an undisputed medical triumph of the COVID era. Also notable, however, is the failure of governments and international organizations to use our current predicament to rectify glaring public health deficiencies.

The Global Health Security Index for 2021 rated the world's 195 countries as "dangerously unprepared" to deal with future epidemic and pandemic threats. The average score for individual countries came in at 38.9 out of 100, about the same as the 2019 rating—before the pandemic began. Many countries failed to grasp that the pandemic presented an unparalleled opportunity to lay the groundwork for coping with not only this public health crisis but also future ones.

Readiness for a COVID-30 or a new pandemic flu strain—or, for that matter, an out-of-control bioweapon—will require new generations of surveillance tools, diagnostics, and drugs, as well as, say, a "universal" coronavirus vaccine that can counter any strain. Having sufficient available vaccine formulations with long shelf lives would also help alleviate the inequities that have accompanied distribution of shots. Underscoring the absence of "global" in "global public health," Portugal had fully vaccinated 89 percent of its population by mid-January but Mali only 2.8 percent.

The most pressing priority should be a return to basics, both globally and locally. COVID has served as a painful demonstration that public health is as essential to national security as a standing army. And the cost of health security is minimal. In 2016 the Commission on a Global Health Risk Framework for the Future estimated that for 65 cents a year for every person on the planet, we could upgrade national pandemic preparedness programs worldwide. An investment of $4.5 billion—far less than the price of a single new ballistic missile submarine—might prevent the global loss of millions of lives and an economic hit in the trillions of dollars.

The basics entail not only building new systems to prepare for pandemics but a major strengthening of institutions already in place. Public health legal expert Lawrence O. Gostin notes in this issue that the World Health Organization has a 2022–2023 budget of $6.12 billion, which is less than those of some major U.S. teaching hospitals. The WHO needs not just money but reforms that give it the authority to better monitor and intervene when new infectious diseases emerge. At the country level, the most basic of basics consist of functioning national systems that furnish medical care for all and financial help, as needed, for child care, food and housing, and other measures to waylay the poverty-related chronic diseases capable of sending even a relatively young adult onto a ventilator during a future pandemic.

After repeated outbreaks of horrific diseases such as SARS, Ebola, and Zika, perhaps this calamity will prove traumatic enough to allow for a coherent remake of the current system. Deaths from COVID worldwide by mid-January about equaled the population of Norway—and the pandemic is still with us. Only when global public health commands the attention of policy makers in the same way as a new contract for nuclear submarines will Greek letters return to their more familiar role in American life as naming conventions for student groups on college campuses.

How Real-World Data Can Help Us Better Prepare for the Next Pandemic

By Joseph Menzin, Peter Neumann

When we look back at the COVID pandemic, what will hindsight tell us? Will we remember the turn of the decade as the year that finally brought real change to pandemic preparedness, or will our eventual return to "normal" stymie our progress?

Although epidemiologists have long warned about the potential for global pandemics, their admonitions have largely gone unheeded. However, industrialized animal farming practices, increased human-animal contact, globalization, decreasing biodiversity, and other factors all point to the likelihood of another zoonotic disease (one transmitted from animals to humans) with pandemic potential .

A slim silver lining of the current COVID-19 pandemic is that it can help us better prepare for future outbreaks–if we harness what we've learned correctly. In particular, we can better leverage one of the most crucial resources we have when it comes to pandemic preparedness: real-world data.

The Importance of Real-Time Insight

The pandemic has created a trove of data that can help us plan for future disease outbreaks. The abundance of research on the U.S. pandemic response provides insight into the benefits and consequences of various courses of action, and we can leverage this knowledge for future response.

One of the main takeaways is the need for the health care system to have real-time visibility. While observers have stated again and again that the ineffective roll-out of testing was (and still is) one of the U.S.'s biggest failings in getting ahead of COVID-19, there is a wealth of other data that can offer insight into the virus' spread. We need to improve in collecting, sharingm and analyzing this real-world data so we can rapidly recognize COVID-19 symptoms, identify effective treatments, and more quickly track the spread.

For example, when the pandemic began, information disseminated by public health organizations identified sore throat, shortness of breath, cough, and fever as symptoms. However, months later additional symptoms like rashes and skin discoloration–such as on the toes and feet–were recognized as potential indicators of the virus. Additionally, what has been termed "silent hypoxia"–COVID-19 causing critically low blood-oxygen levels without any noticeable external effects on breathing–killed many patients before doctors knew to be on the lookout for it.

Why weren't we able to recognize these symptoms sooner? The electronic health records (EHRs) in which physicians document patient visits do not allow for an easy, effective way for data to be shared at scale. If de-identified patient data could be mined at a national level, artificial intelligence and machine-learning algorithms could have identified patterns far faster than it took isolated researchers working with small patient pools. Instead of examining COVID-19 data holistically, within six months, researchers had published over 23,500 papers–a wealth of information, but too much data for any one individual to possibly parse through and identify the valuable studies.

Centralizing data access could have not only sped the identification of COVID symptoms but also allowed for rapid studies of effective treatments. Researchers could use a truly robust database to analyze and identify which treatments are most effective for patients with various underlying conditions or disease histories.

Furthermore, using machine-learning techniques within a shared database could generate predictive insights, showing the patterns in communities that precede outbreaks and helping dictate where and when lockdowns and social distancing orders should be implemented. Several countries are already using unconventional data sources, like de-identified cell phone and fitness tracking data, to predict COVID outbreaks. For example, Germany is using de-identified tracking apps to identify anomalies in day-to-day habits, such as regularly active users skipping exercising or walks to predict when a community is likely about to experience an outbreak–and prevent it before it worsens.

The experience of Israel offers a great example of how real-world data can be analyzed and shared. By swiftly rolling out the Pfizer vaccine to more than half its population and tracking the results, the country was able to demonstrate a dramatic decrease in serious infections and hospitalizations as a consequence of the vaccine. This real-world evidence is key to understanding how the vaccine works outside the confines of controlled clinical trials and in much larger populations.

These measures represent just the basics of what policy makers can do to inform real-time insights. And the benefits need not be used just for pandemic preparedness; mining and analyzing de-identified data could be used to identify effective strategies for fighting any number of conditions, from mental health concerns to chronic illnesses.

Hindsight, Foresight, and Insight

When the next novel virus with pandemic potential inevitably arises, the changes and preparations we put in place in the coming months and years will determine if we can better manage another crisis on the scale of COVID-19. Urgent action must be taken, as our health care system continues to experience breakdowns of data sharing at every level. While COVID-19 testing has increased dramatically, organizations still struggle to share test results, as some facilities still rely on fax machines to communicate timely information. When fighting an ongoing pandemic, results delivered weeks after testing serve little purpose in preventing the spread of disease. We must enable real-time insight and recognize the importance of studying past events if we are to have the foresight to prevent the next pandemic.

While some countries, like the U.K., have dedicated significant resources to sequencing additional COVID-19 genomes, the U.S.

is 32nd in the world for the number of sequences completed per 1,000 COVID cases. The inability not only to identify the mutated virus, but also to easily recognize any significant shifts in virus epidemiology at that level, will continue to hamper our ability to predict and prevent spread.

While there will always be differing opinions on the best course of action for pandemic preparedness and prevention, we need to create a more effective forum for discussion and must continue to encourage discourse between many disciplines to weigh the potential social, economic, and physiological ramifications of various courses. These discussions should not wait until the next pandemic arrives. Instead, we must establish and fully fund think tanks and committees to imagine possible scenarios and responses.

We should seek to answer important questions, such as: How long can businesses of various socioeconomic levels survive closures, and what type of aid is most effective? What are the long-term implications of a child missing a year of school or attending school virtually? How does isolation affect mental health among people of different age groups, income levels, and urban and rural settings, and what strategies work to mitigate these effects? What lessons can be learned from countries with sophisticated data capture systems?

With the right data to analyze–and the right experts to analyze such data–we are fully capable of answering these questions and gathering the necessary insights to understand the ongoing impact of COVID-19. Armed with this knowledge and with a global recognition of the consequences of an ineffective response, we'll have the motivation and means to take the appropriate precautions and prevent a future pandemic before it starts.

This is an opinion and analysis article.

About the Author

Joseph Menzin, Ph.D., is the CEO and founder of Panalgo, a health care analytics company.

GLOSSARY

antigen Any substance foreign to the body that evokes an immune response.

antibodies Proteins that are produced by the body in order to fight antigens as part of an immune response.

dilapidated In very bad condition due to age, neglect, or misuse

epidemiology The study of how disease spreads and can be controlled.

epinephrine A medication used in emergencies to treat life-threatening allergic reactions to insect bites, foods, drugs, or other substances.

human papillomavirus A group of related viruses that can cause warts on different parts of the body and is spread through intimate skin-to-skin contact.

immunology A science that studies the ways in which the human body protects itself from diseases and infections.

immunotherapy A treatment or prevention of disease that involves the stimulation, enhancement, or suppression of the immune system.

microbes Extremely small living things that can only be seen with a microscope.

pathogen Something, such as a bacteria or virus, that causes disease.

placebo A pill or substance that is given to a patient like a drug but has no physical effect on the patient.

polio A life-threatening infectious disease common in children that can infect a person's spinal cord, causing paralysis.

Tuskegee Institute A private, historically African-American university founded in 1881 and located in Tuskegee, Alabama.

FURTHER INFORMATION

Hodson, Richard. "Autoimmune disease," *Nature*, 14 July 2022, https://www.nature.com/articles/d41586-021-01833-y

Holmes, Bob. "Should Traditional Vaccines Be Used in the Global Fight Against Covid?" *Smithsonian Magazine*, 22 April 2022, https://www.smithsonianmag.com/science-nature/should-traditional-vaccines-be-used-to-help-protect-the-world-against-covid-180979950/

"How Do Vaccines Work?" World Health Organization, 8 December 2020, https://www.who.int/news-room/feature-stories/detail/how-do-vaccines-work

Kluger, Jeff. "A Vaccine Against COVID-19 Would Be the Latest Success in a Long Scientific History," Time, 15 May 2020, https://time.com/5835668/vaccine-history/

Mayo Clinic Staff. "Flu shot: Your best bet for avoiding influenza," Mayo Clinic, 10 September 2021, https://www.mayoclinic.org/diseases-conditions/flu/in-depth/flu-shots/art-20048000

Meissner, H. Cody. "Understanding Vaccine Safety and the Roles of the FDA and the CDC," *The New England Journal of Medicine*, 28 April 2022, https://www.nejm.org/doi/full/10.1056/NEJMra2200583

Schmidt, Charles. "'When Will Kids under Five Get COVID Vaccines?' and Other Questions," *Scientific American*, 24 May 2022, https://www.scientificamerican.com/article/when-will-kids-under-five-get-covid-vaccines-and-other-questions/

Simpson, J. Cavanaugh. "The Man Who Beat the 1957 Flu Pandemic," *Scientific American*, 19 April 2020, https://blogs.scientificamerican.com/observations/the-man-who-beat-the-1957-flu-pandemic/

Wetzel, Corryn. "First Woman Has Been 'Cured' of HIV Using Stem Cells," *Smithsonian Magazine*, 22 February 2022, https://www.smithsonianmag.com/smart-news/first-woman-has-been-cured-of-hiv-using-stem-cells-180979614/

CITATIONS

1.1 How to Boost Your Immunity by Claudia Wallis (July 1, 2020); 1.2 Fact or Fiction: Vaccines Are Dangerous by Dina Fine Maron (March 6, 2015); 1.3 The Brain Has a Special Kind of Memory for Past Infections by Raleigh MsElvery (November 8, 2021); 1.4 Hidden Black Scientists Proved the Polio Vaccine Worked by Ainissa Ramirez (June 17, 2021); 1.5 Vaccines Reimagined by Melinda Wenner Moyer (June 1, 2019); 1.6 Genomic Vaccines Fight Disease in Ways Not Possible Before by Geoffrey Ling (June 26, 2017); 2.1 How I Was Betrayed from Within by Maria Konnikova (September 1, 2021); 2.2 The Terrible Toll of 76 Autoimmune Diseases by Maddie Bender, Jen Christiansen, Miriam Quick (September 1, 2021); 2.3 Targeted Treatments for Autoimmune Disease Make Progress by Marla Broadfoot (September 1, 2021); 2.4 How Blood Sugar Can Trigger a Deadly Immune Response in the Flu and Possibly COVID-19 by Claudia Wallis (April 24, 2020); 2.5 How to Kill HIV: Target Its "Influencers" by Apoorva Mandavilli (May 2, 2019); 3.1 A Shot Against Cancer by Karen Weintraub (April 1, 2016); 3.2 Are We Innately Immune to Cancer by Mark Lowdell (January 24, 2019); 3.3 What's Next after Creating a Cancer-Prevention Vaccine by Dina Fine Maron (September 6, 2017); 3.4 Could Immunotherapy Treat Diseases Besides Cancer? by Karen Weintraub (September 30, 2019); 3.5 Fighting the Opioid Crisis with Vaccines and Better Chemistry by Dina Fine Maron (August 17, 2017); 3.6 The Next Wave of Immuno-Oncology by Rafael Amado (May 20, 2019); 3.7 Vanquishing Diabetes by Kristen M. Drescher & Steven Tracy (February 1, 2018); 3.8 Immune Cells Suggest New Alzheimer's Treatment Possibilities by Jason Ulrich, David M. Holtzman (August 1, 2021); 4.1 A Visual Guide to the SARS-CoV-2 Coronavirus by Mark Fischetti, Veronica Falconieri Hays, Britt Glaunsinger, Jen Christiansen (July 1, 2020); 4.2 What Immunity to COVID-19 Really Means by Stacey McKenna (April 10, 2020); 4.3 COVID-19 Vaccine Developers Search for Antibodies that "First Do No Harm" by Esther Landhuis (May 28, 2020); 4.4 Fast-Track Drugs by Michael Waldholz (June 1, 2020); 5.1 How Communication around COVID Fuels a Mistrust of Science by Joseph V. Sakran, Kavita K. Patel (January 6, 2022); 5.2 The Vaccine Rollout Is Changing How We Think about Prescription Meds by Mark Westall (May 26, 2021); 5.3 We Need a Universal Flu Vaccine before the Next Pandemic Strikes by Catharine I. Paules & Anthony S. Fauci (February 1, 2018); 5.4 Contagions Worse Than COVID Will Prevail If Neglect of Global Public Health Continues by The Editors (March 1, 2022); 5.5 How Real-World Data Can Help Us Better Prepare for the Next Pandemic by Joseph Menzin, Peter Neumann (April 22, 2021)

Each author biography was accurate at the time the article was originally published.

INDEX